CH00767456

POWER TOOLS FOR HOME AND GARDEN

POWER TOOLS FOR HOME AND GARDEN
A Do-it-yourself Handbook

FREDERICK PURVES

Published in association with
Black & Decker Ltd.

LONDON

BLANDFORD PRESS

ISBN 0 7137 0561 2

Acknowledgements
The author and publishers wish to record
their appreciation of the help they have
received from the Black & Decker
organisation in preparing this book. In
particular they are grateful for the
personal interest of Mr S. A. Ryall,
Director of Advertising, and Mr 'Bill'
Richardson, Sales Training Manager, who
kindly read the manuscript.
They wish also to thank Mr David Johnson,
Managing Editor, *Do-it-yourself Magazine,*
for checking the text and making many
constructive suggestions which the author
has been happy to incorporate.

Typeset by H. Charlesworth and Co. Ltd.,
    Huddersfield, Yorkshire
Printed by Redwood Press Ltd.,
    Trowbridge, Wiltshire

CONTENTS

to use the finishing sander

THE POWER TOOL REVOLUTION

Man is a tool-using animal. As long as there have been men there have been tools, but up to recent years they have always been basically the same. When the Ancient Egyptians built the pyramids they used drills, saws, chisels, planes and hammers that were cruder than the ones we use today, but not all that different. A man from Mars wouldn't have any trouble in pairing up the tools used by workmen centuries before the Romans came to Britain with their modern equivalents.

But over the last 20 years or so the whole picture has changed. The revolution actually started earlier than that when the first electrically powered portable drill arrived on the market, but like Aladdin's lamp it lay around for a long time before its real powers were appreciated.

At first the electric drill was just a handy gadget for boring holes in wood and metal. Then it was gradually realised that the new tool was more than a drill; it was a versatile power unit that could transform all the traditional operations of shaping and finishing: it could step up the speed and scope of the whole range of hand tools for both the home handyman and the craftsman. Once this became clear, the industry lost no time in developing bigger and better motors to drive a new generation of individual power tools and power drill attachments for circular sawing, jig sawing, sanding, turning, finishing, planing and shaping. The result is that simply by pressing a switch and guiding a tool you can now do the sort of job that once called for specialised skills which took craftsmen years to acquire. In most cases, by using the proper tool you can do a quicker, better job with only a fraction of the effort.

The power tool revolution has come as a blessing in all sorts of ways apart from the actual work it does. Whether it is a good thing or not, we are all frantically packing more and more different activities into our waking hours and we have less and less spare time for the things we want to do. Power tools help us to get more done in a shorter time so we can get more out of our hobbies, we can create or construct more of the things we want to furnish our homes and gardens and we can save both time and money on repairs in the house, garage and garden.

There was a time when you could get the odd job done or a bit of woodwork knocked up for a shilling or two that you didn't miss. Those days are gone, for better or for worse. Nowadays it is either impossible to get anybody to do an occasional job, or you have to pay more than it's worth to get it done for you. So today you can easily save the cost of a power tool on the first job you do with it.

When you come to the end of the measurable benefits of owning one or more power tools, there is still what for some users is the best reason of all—whether they admit it to themselves or not. It is that power tools are fun. The thrill of feeling a drill go whistling through a chunk of wood or of being able to rip—saw at high speed through a plank is something that never fades, however often you do it.

Psychologists say we enjoy using power tools because they help us to get rid of nervous tensions and give expression to the creative urge present in most human beings. But that is just another way of saying that they are fun to use and just another proof that we never get tired of playing with toys. The classic picture of complete relaxation has always been the man sitting on a log, whittling a piece of wood. The picture is still the same, all we have to do to bring it up to date is to substitute a power tool for the penknife.

So much for the background, but if power tools make it all so easy, is there any need for a book about them? Well, like a lot of other things, it's easy only when you know how, and this book is designed to tell you all you need to know about choosing and using power tools to get the best out of them without wasting time and money finding out for yourself the hard way. Don't forget, the power in power tools can be dangerous unless you know how to control it, so it's as well to learn how while you can count the benefits on a full set of fingers.

There are many makes of power tool on the market and most manufacturers offer the attachments which enable you to convert your drill into a range of other tools. Many of these attachments are interchangeable between the different makes of power tool—but not all. The really comprehensive picture could be confusing, so this book is based primarily on the products of one manufacturer, Black & Decker, the world's biggest manufacturer of power tools. They make something like 95 out of every 100 power tools sold over the counter, so the chances are that you either own a Black & Decker power tool already or will eventually buy one. However, as the basic principles are the same for all power tools, all the practical information in this book will apply, no matter which make of power tool you own or buy in the future.

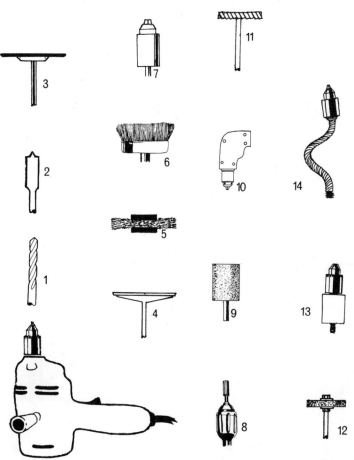

Here are some of the tools that you can fix in the chuck of the basic power tool: 1— twist drill, 2—flat bit, 3— sanding pad, 4— sanding plate, 5— wheel brush, 6— cup brush, 7— speed reducer, 8— screwdriver, 9— drum sander, 10— right angle drilling attachment, 11— paint stirrer, 12— grinding wheel, 13— impact drilling attachment, 14— flexible drive.

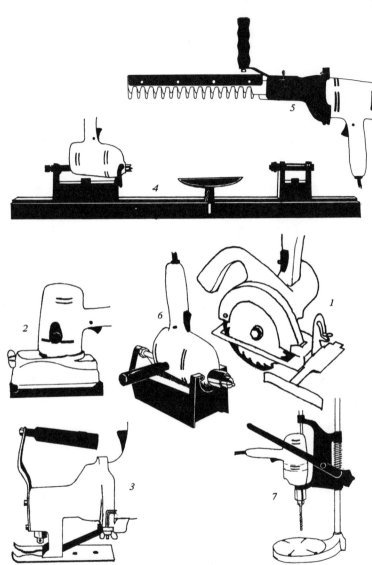

Here are some of the attachments which turn your power drill into another kind of tool: 1— circular saw, 2— orbital sander, 3— jigsaw, 4— lathe, 5— hedge trimmer, 6— horizontal bench stand, 7— vertical bench stand.

POWER DRILLS

Most people start their power tool kit with an electric drill. Later they either buy attachments for converting it to do other jobs or they 'go the whole hog' and buy individual power tools—circular saw, jigsaw and so on and keep their drill as a drill and nothing else. Let's start with the electric drill.

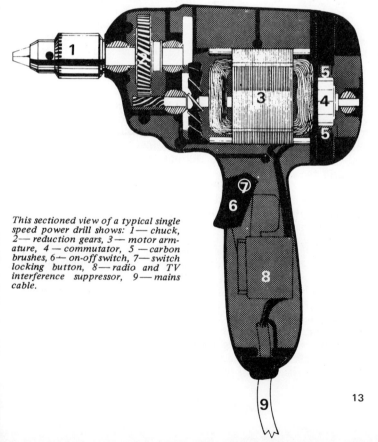

This sectioned view of a typical single speed power drill shows: 1— chuck, 2— reduction gears, 3 — motor armature, 4 — commutator, 5 —carbon brushes, 6— on-off switch, 7— switch locking button, 8— radio and TV interference suppressor, 9— mains cable.

The first thing to notice is that it packs a mighty lot of power into a very small space. This quart-into-pint-pot miracle is made possible by using a very small light weight electric motor which makes up for its small size by running at a high speed. In that way you can get a lot of power out of a small motor (even the cheapest Black & Decker drill develops as much as 1/3 horse power). If you connect the drill directly to the motor it will run much too fast for most drilling jobs, so you have to step down the speed of the motor shaft to match the lower working speed of the drill. This is generally done by building a gearbox in to the drill between the motor and the chuck—the holder that grips the drill that actually does the boring of the holes.

Now you have an idea of the basic make-up of the ordinary electric drill. You have a high speed electric motor with a small gear wheel on the end of its shaft. This gearwheel drives a much bigger one connected directly to the chuck. With this arrangement the little wheel has to turn round many times to make the big one turn round only once, so while the motor is fairly whizzing around, the drill turns at its proper working speed which is much slower. This enables you to bore a hole or make a saw cut without overloading the motor or over-heating and blunting the cutting edge of the tool.

There is another extremely important piece of hardware incorporated in the motor: the cooling fan. This tiny component is mounted on the high speed spindle of the motor and draws a stream of cold air around the electrical windings, through slits in the back of the drill case and blows it out through another set of slits at the front end of the case. Without this continuous flow of fresh air through the drill the electrical windings would quickly get overheated and burn out. You can now see the danger of overloading the drill to the point where the motor speed drops to a few hundred revolutions per minute. At that speed the fan is practically useless and you run the risk of burning out the windings.

During a spell of hard drilling, if you think the tool is getting hot, let it run idle for a minute or two with the motor turning at its maximum speed. The fan will quickly lower the temperature and, you can safely press on with the job again.

The motor and gearbox are mounted in a light alloy or specially tough plastics case with a pistol grip handle and an on-off trigger switch placed where your fore-finger finds it naturally, as it would the trigger of a gun. The drill chuck sticks out in front like the barrel of the gun. There's a lot in common between holding and firing a pistol and drilling a hole with a hand-held electric power tool, so the similarity of the grip, 'barrel' and trigger makes sense. As most power tools get their electricity supply from the mains, you have a length of cable connected to the drill with a plug on the end for connecting it to a power socket.

SIZE AND POWER

Black & Decker, like most of the other power tool manufacturers, offer a range of power tools from small low cost models for the occasional user and hobbyist to the husky work-horses used in industry. The usual way of classifying the tools in a particular range is by stating the diameter of the biggest drill that you can grip in the chuck. A 1/4 in. power tool has a chuck that will hold a 1/4 in. drill and a 1/2 in. tool will take a 1/2 in. diameter drill. The drill size here refers to the size of the drill shank held in the chuck. This is the same size as the hole made by a drill designed for metal but in drills designed for wood the actual business end and the hole it drills may be bigger—e.g., you can get a drill for drilling a 1/2 in. hole in wood with a shank only 1/4 in. in diameter so that it can fit a 1/4 in. drill chuck. (For more detailed information see What You Need, p. 24.)

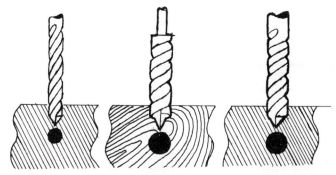

Left: a 1/4 in. power tool will only take a 1/4 in. parallel twist drill for drilling metal, but by using a stepped shank drill you can drill 1/2 in. holes - but only in wood. Right: Drilling 1/2 in. holes in metal calls for a more powerful tool fitted with a 1/2 in. chuck.

It takes more power to drill a 1/2 in. hole in either wood or metal than it does to drill a hole only half the diameter in the same material, so the size and drilling capacity of a power drill get bigger along with the size of the chuck. Of course, the price increases too; you expect to pay more for a 3/8 in. tool than a 5/16 in. model in the same manufacturer's range.

In addition to the standard rating—1/4 in., 3/8 in., 1/2 in. etc.— the manufacturer usually tells you the capacity of the tool for drilling other materials, e.g., 3/8 in. in steel, 1/2 in. in masonry, 3/4 in. in wood. This figure indicates the capacity of the drill—not the size of the chuck. In the case just quoted the 1/2 in. masonry and 3/4 in. wood drills must still have a shank of 3/8 in. diameter or less before they can be gripped in the 3/8 in. drill chuck. The drill manufacturers make a range of drills of this type specially for portable power drills.

SPEED

The speed of the chuck is as important as its size and you have to know something about both before you can say what a particular drill will do. It takes about four times as much power to drill a 1/2 in. hole as to drill one only 1/4 in. in diameter if you want it to drill through the same thickness of material in the same time. However, if you gear the 1/2 in. drill down to 1/4 the speed it will drill out the same amount of material as the 1/4 in. drill in the same time. If you do that, you won't need any more power to drive the big drill than you need to drive the smaller one, but you will have to put up with the slower rate of drilling. In other words, the big drill will take four times as long to get through the same thickness of metal as the small one, but of course the hole will be 1/2 in. instead of only 1/4 in.

If you want to drill bigger holes or harder materials, you can either use the same size motor, geared down to work at a slower rate, or pay for a drill with a more powerful motor and cut the drilling time. Either way you finish up with a more expensive drill, but of the two ways, the cheaper is to gear the motor down because fitting a bigger motor means increasing the size of everything. Of course, if you want the best of both worlds, you can have a more powerful motor and gear it down as well for really tough work. However, that still is not the end of the story if you are trying to work out which type of power tool will be best for your particular purpose. You have to think about the material you are most likely to be drilling.

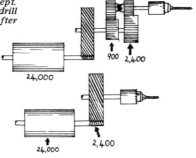

A 2-speed drill gives you a choice of 2 gear ratios, providing a high speed for fast drilling of small holes and soft materials and a low speed for larger holes and harder materials.

You can drill holes in metal up to the diameter of the largest parallel shank drill the chuck will accept. You can use a stepped shank drill for making larger holes in softer materials.

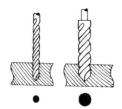

A single speed drill has a simple speed reduction gearbox which provides one chuck speed for all materials.

Every material—steel, wood, masonry, plastics, glass, ceramics, aluminium, asbestos—has a maximum cutting speed. This depends on the hardness of the material and its resistance to being cut and also on the speed at which it conducts away the heat set up by the cutting action of the tool. If the heat set up at the cutting edge of the drill is not conducted away fast enough by the material around the hole, sooner or later it will build up to a situation where the point of the drill gets dangerously hot. When that happens the steel softens, the drill loses its edge and stops cutting.

There is a maximum safe cutting speed for every material. (It doesn't matter whether you are cutting it with a drill, a saw, a turning tool or a milling cutter, the maximum cutting speed of the tool for that material is the same.) If you are a production engineer you try to machine every material at its maximum speed because a slower speed would waste machining capacity and a higher speed means that you are continually stopping to replace worn-out cutters.

Once you know the maximum cutting speed for the material you can work out how fast the drill must turn so that the outside edge of the drill will cut at that speed. (The outside edge is the fastest moving part of the drill; if that is not cutting too fast then the slower moving parts of the edge nearer the centre will be well on the safe side.)

For example, if the recommended speed for cutting mild steel is 120 ft per minute and you want to drill a 1/2 in. hole in it, then the outside edge of the drill must not travel at more than 120 ft per minute. The circumference of a 1/2 in. hole is very roughly 1 1/2 in.; so the outside edge of the drill travels this distance in every revolution, and in travelling 120 ft it must turn 120 ft × 12 ÷ 1.5 in. times. To do this once every minute the drill must turn at a speed of 960 r.p.m. (revolutions per minute).

However exact calculations like that only make sense if you are dealing with a machine that is cutting one material all the time, as on a production line in a factory. When you buy a power tool for your home workshop you want it to cut holes of different sizes in all sorts of materials, so you have to compromise. The alternatives are, either to buy a number of separate power tools with speeds to suit the various materials you want to drill, or to buy one drill with some means of changing the speed to match the material. You can also buy a compact little gear box that you can add to your power drill to reduce its speed by about 4 : 1 when necessary—e.g. for drilling holes in masonry or extra large holes in wood.

Some people choose one way and some another, the important thing is to make the choice with your eyes open and not just rush into the business and wish you had bought something different when it's too late. What you have read so far is aimed at helping you to make the right choice in the first place. You are now less likely to buy a model that is not strong enough to stand up to the heavy programme of work you have in mind and on the other hand you will not spend good money on extra features that you are not likely to use.

This is a good place to take a closer look at the options open to you when you are choosing a power drill for the first time. What are the pluses and minuses of the single speed general purpose drills, the drills that give you a choice of fixed speeds and the ones with a speed control that takes you smoothly from zero to full speed and enables you to work at any speed you choose in between?

SINGLE SPEED MODELS

As you would expect, there are more single speed power drills sold than any other kind. This is because they are cheaper to buy and easier to use. You do not have to wonder which speed to use if your drill only has one.

Most single speed power drills, including those in the Black & Decker range, run at around 2,500 r.p.m. and the sizes range from 1/4 in. to 3/8 in. although in recent years the 1/4 in. size has mostly been dropped in favour of the 5/16 in. These tools are suitable for drilling holes in steel up to the maximum jaw diameter of the chuck and to proportionately larger diameters in masonry and wood: 3/8 in. and 5/8 in. (5/16 in. drill); 1/2 in. and 3/4 in. (3/8 in. drill).

The speed of the chuck printed on the name plate of the power tool refers to the no-load condition. When the drill is actually working it slows down. You can easily check this for yourself by drilling a piece of scrap iron or hardwood. Listen to the sound of the drill before you apply any pressure and then notice how the note drops pitch as you press harder and the drill bites deeper. Up to a point, this drop in speed is normal and is all cared for in the design of the tool, but, as the drill works harder and the speed falls, the current through the motor rises, producing more heat in the electrical windings. At the very time when you could do with extra cooling, the fan on the motor runs slower and carries away less heat than usual, the tool starts to feel hot and if you ignore the warning something is apt to melt or burn and you may seriously damage the motor. (If you notice the drill overheating the right thing is to withdraw it from the hole but keep the switch pressed. This way the speed of the motor rises and the fan cools it down much faster than if you simply switch off the tool.)

However, if you are prepared to work within the limits of speed and power of the tool, the single speed drill is capable of doing a truly surprising number of useful jobs both as a drill, pure and simple, and in conjunction with a range of attachments for sanding, sawing, wood turning and so on. (These attachments are dealt with later.)

The average home handyman will be able to do most of the normal 'make and mend' jobs around the house with a single speed power tool. After all, for a long time it was the only type available and it laid the foundation of the whole range of tools and attachments that have been developed as a result of its popularity. At the present time there are several million tools of this type in use in Great Britain alone.

Throughout this book you can take it for granted that everything dealing with the use of power tools or attachments applies to the single speed tool unless otherwise stated.

If you list all the jobs you might want to do with a portable power tool you would find that 95 out of 100 can be carried out either between 200—300 r.p.m. at the slow speed end of the list or 2,000—3,000 r.p.m. at the high speed end. This is a pretty full order for a single speed tool and although you have a lot of latitude above and below the ideal speeds for most jobs, you can get closer to the ideal if you have two speeds to choose from. It is especially useful to have a speed in the lower region for the really tough jobs like drilling in steel, masonry and driving big holes through wood. This sort of job puts a heavy load on the drill motor, like driving a car up a steep hill. If the hill is too steep for the car it stalls and leaves you stuck in the middle, but when the load is too big for your power tool, stalling could mean burning out the motor and a large bill for repairs. In each case the answer is to drop down into a lower gear, and while your car needs 3 or 4 speeds you can go a long way with a 2-speed power tool.

Black & Decker have selected 900 r.p.m. and 2,400 r.p.m. as the two most useful speeds for their 2-speed drills. Any jobs calling for drill speeds between say 200 and 1,000 r.p.m. can be taken care of by the low speed and all the rest from 1,000 up to 3,000 by the high speed.

With a 2-speed model you have a high speed for such things as drilling wood, and driving saws, sanders, a wood-turning lathe and other high speed attachments and you have a low speed for drilling large holes or tough materials and for polishing, and driving hole saws, screwdrivers and nut runners. Later on in the book when you read about the various drill attachments and their power requirements, you will be able to decide whether you need the extra luxury of a 2-speed drill or whether a single speed model will do all you want; but you will be wise to think hard before deciding because it can be irritating to find yourself making allowances for a tool that isn't really capable of the job.

Black & Decker drills are made in 3/8 in. and 1/2 in. sizes. The 3/8 in. drill has a capacity of 3/8 in. in steel, 1/2 in. in masonry and 3/4 in. in wood. The 1/2 in. drills have a capacity of 1/2 in. in steel, 3/4 in. in masonry and 1 in. in wood. These drills are for the really serious handyman and used by craftsmen joiners and for industrial purposes.

VARIABLE SPEED MODELS

A few years ago the electronics industry came up with a new sort of transistor that made it possible to control electrical equipment such as lighting, heaters and motors, continuously from zero to full power without having to waste what they were not actually using. Previously you could always dim out lighting or slow down a motor by turning part of the power into waste heat, but now for the first time you could control, say, the speed of a motor all the way from rest to top speed without wasting power.

This useful gadget, called a thyristor, is the basis of special Black & Decker power drills which have a continuously variable range of speeds that you select simply by finger pressure on the trigger—the further you pull it back the faster the drill turns. In many ways this is the ideal form of control because you can select the exact speed to suit the diameter of the drill and the nature of the material you are drilling.

There are two types of Black & Decker drill with thyristor control, one is the normal single speed drill and the other a 2-speed model. You may wonder what advantage there is in adding a 2-speed gearbox to a drill which already has complete and continuous control over the whole range of motor speeds. The answer is that for many of the jobs where you want a slow speed you still want as much power as possible. The thyristor control slows down the speed by restricting the power; if you want to slow down the drill without cutting down the power, you have to use a gearbox which makes it possible for the motor to run at a fast speed while the drill turns at the slower speed required by the work in hand.

If you are in doubt about which type to buy (and naturally the geared model costs more), then these are the things you have to bear in mind: the 2-speed model in fast gear and the single speed model have the same type of performance. You can slow them both down to a crawl for drilling difficult materials like glass and ceramic tiles, and you can ease off the speed in the same way at critical times, e.g. when starting a hole or when the drill breaks through the other side of the material which you are drilling. You will also get the same performance with all the high speed attachments. Up to this point there is nothing to choose between the models. You only start to notice the difference when you want maximum power at the slow speeds, e.g. for drilling large diameter holes in steel and masonry, or with some of the attachments like polishers and grinders and the wood turning lathe that take a proportionately large amount of power to drive them. This is where it is useful to be able to change to the lower gear and have something like three times the power to play with. Remember that when you run the single speed drill at a reduced speed, the cooling fan slows down also and there is more risk of overheating and damaging the motor. However, Black &

Decker power tools are designed for hard work and even the single speed drills will stand up to a surprising amount of heavy use, so unless you have a special reason for choosing the 2-speed model, the single speed model will almost certainly do all you want.

2-SPEED HAMMER DRILL

The hammer drill is designed for one specific job—drilling holes in concrete and masonry. In the normal way you can make holes in brickwork and mortar with one of the special tungsten carbide tipped masonry drills sold for the purpose (p 40). But concrete is an extra tough proposition because it contains flint-like aggregate which is too hard even for a tungsten carbide tool to cut. The only way to deal with this is to shatter it. In the past holes were cut in concrete with a hammer and a steel rod sharpened to a pyramid-shaped point and hardened. By hammering on the end of the rod and turning it between blows the flints could be broken up and a hole made. To make a neat accurate job you should use a lot of light blows with the hammer and turn the drill between every blow. Most people try to speed up the operation by hitting the drill hard and not bothering to turn it. The result is that instead of a nice clean hole you get a very rough affair and by banging away with the hammer you generally crack the surrounding surface and damage any plastering or rendering.

The Black & Decker hammer drill is a 2-speed drill with a difference. By turning a collar between the chuck and the body of the drill you change the rotary motion of the chuck into a succession of high speed hammer blows—up to 40,000 per minute. This action is just what you want to nibble away at the very hard aggregate and turn it into powder without a lot of banging and crashing. The action is the same as that of the bigger industrial hammer drills made by the company but it has been adapted to a normal 2-speed drill so that you have the benefit of two separate tools for little more than the price of one. Obviously this is the model to buy if you are likely to be doing a lot of work on masonry, such as putting up heavy duty shelving, fastening things down to concrete floors or adding extensions to the house, garage, tool shed or garden buildings.

HOW TO REMOVE THE DRILL CHUCK

The chuck of a Black & Decker power drill can be unscrewed from its driving spindle so that you can fit other accessories and attachments in its place and use the drill to power them.

This is how you remove the chuck:

1 Hold the drill in your left hand or lay it on the bench pointing away from you.

2 Fit the drill key into one of the three holes in the nose and turn the chuck until the stem of the key sticks straight out to the right.

3 Hold the drill firmly and tap the stem of the chuck key smartly downwards with a light hammer or, better still, a wooden mallet or block of wood. This will slacken the chuck on its thread.

4 Unscrew the chuck by hand and screw in the drive adaptor or other accessory. Check that there is a fibre washer fitted to the threaded part to make it easy to unscrew when you want to remove it and replace the chuck.

The drive adaptor is easily unscrewed. Grip the projecting blade with an adjustable spanner and loosen it with a tap on the handle of the spanner as you did with the chuck key when removing the chuck.

To remove the chuck so that you can screw other accessories in its place: point the power tool away from you, fit the chuck key on the right hand side and strike it sharply downwards with a block of wood or a soft faced hammer.

If you are likely to be taking the handle off frequently it is a good idea to pack a wad of paper into the hollow moulding to keep the head of the bolt in place. You can always remove it if necessary by tapping the bolt end on the bench to drive the paper wad out.

THE SIDE HANDLE

A moulded handle is supplied with most general purpose power drills for home use. These tools are designed so that they can be used to power attachments of various types, so the shape has to be a compromise which allows it to be either clamped to an attachment or bench stand or used as a hand-held drill which you need to hold with both hands. This is where you need an extra hand grip because if you hold on to the body of the drill with one hand you have not the same control and you can easily block the ventilation slits with your hand and overheat the motor.

The handle supplied with the Black & Decker power tools is a hollow moulding held on to the body of the tool by a hexagon-headed bolt which engages with a shaped recess in the bottom end of the hole. The easiest way to fit it is to drop the bolt into the hole in the handle and then keep the head engaged with the hexagonal recess in the bottom with a pencil or a screwdriver. You can then tighten the bolt by turning the handle. You can screw the handle into either side of the tool or remove it altogether when you are using attachments which have their own extra handle, like the circular saw and jig saw attachments, or which do not need an extra handle, like the lathe attachment and the vertical and horizontal drill stands.

USING YOUR POWER DRILL

Nowadays you can do a complete range of jobs with a power drill in addition to drilling holes, but as drilling holes is its main function, the first thing you want to know about power tools is how to do simple drilling operations. Soon you will want to know about the various attachments you can add to your power drill for sawing, sanding, wood turning and so on. When you do you will find full information under the separate sections on tools and attachments for sawing, sanding etc. Any other gadgets you can use with your drill—e.g. for drilling at right angles, working a compressor for a paint spray gun, dovetailing, rebating and other specialised jobs you will find in the chapter on Extras to Help You. This chapter is about the basic operation of drilling holes in all sorts of materials.

WHAT YOU NEED
As well as your power drill, you are going to need a set of drills and the sort you buy will depend on the material you want to drill. The drills you need for metal are not the same as the ones you should use for wood or masonry or glass and tiles. Most people will want to drill both metal and wood, and that means buying two kinds of drill. For metal you use twist drills and for wood, auger bits.

A twist drill for metal is a rod of the same diameter from the plain end that you grip in the chuck, to the fluted end with the sharpened edges that drill the hole. You cannot fit a metal drill bigger than the chuck size—ie a 3/8 in. chuck will take a 3/8 in. diameter metal drill but nothing bigger. When you buy a drill for metal you have a choice of two kinds of steel: carbon or high speed. If you're going to do a lot of drilling into metal, particularly tough steel, you should pay the extra for high speed drills; but if you only need to drill metal either occasionally, or in nothing harder than aluminium, the cheaper carbon steel drills are all you need. For a start, with a 3/8 in. diameter power tool you should buy a set of drills consisting of at least 1/8 in., 3/16 in., 1/4 in. and 3/8 in. You are more likely to need the 3/8 in. drill if you have a 2-speed tool, but with care you can use one of this size to drill steel even with a single speed model.

An auger bit for drilling wood has a much wider fluted spiral to clear away the bigger wood chips. The business end has a pointed screw in the centre and a sharp knife blade at the outside of the cutting edge. The knife blade makes a circular slit in the surface before the cutting edge of the drill makes contact and starts removing the wood. This ensures a clean edge to the hole. Auger bits are

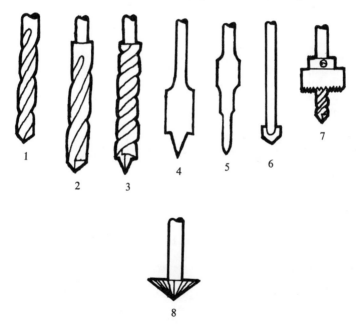

Here are the principal types of drill for use in your power tool: 1— parallel shank twist drill for metal and wood, 2 & 3 — stepped shank drills for larger holes in wood etc., 4— flat bit for wood, 5 — combination pilot, clearance and countersink bits for wood, 6 — tipped drill for masonry, tiles and glass 7 — holesaw for plywood or sheet metal and plastics, 8— countersink bit.

made with shanks to suit the size of your drill chuck irrespective of the size of hole they drill.

The centre point of an auger bit designed for use in a carpenter's brace has a sharp-edged coarse thread which pulls the bit into the wood. The same type of bit when used in a power tool has no need for a threaded centre point—in fact the thread would tend to pull the bit into the wood too quickly. If you want to use such a bit in your power tool you should grind or file away the thread, leaving only a smooth centre point.

You can drill holes in wood with metal cutting drills so there is no point in buying auger bits smaller than the size of your largest metal cutting drill. So, if your biggest metal cutting drill is 3/8 in. diameter and your power drill is rated up to 3/4 in. in wood, you should start with 1/2 in. and 3/4 in. auger bits, using your metal cutting twist drills for smaller holes.

Long auger bits are usually expensive but if you want to drill very deep holes in wood you can use a much cheaper type of drill bit called a flat bit. This has a long shank with a flat head the width corresponding to the hole size, ground to form two sharp cutting edges with a central point. You can also buy a special type of flat bit with interchangeable cutters in a set usually ranging in 1/8 in. steps from 3/8 in. to 1 in. diameter. However, this type, although cheaper than an equivalent range of individual flat bits can be dangerous if the head comes loose while the drill is rotating.

Flat bits do not give as clean a finish to the hole as the spiral auger bits, but they are useful for cutting long holes which do not have to provide an accurate fit for another component—e.g. for drilling through joists and other constructional woodwork to take electric cables.

You will need one more kind of bit before you start using your power drill seriously. This is a countersink bit which you use to recess the opening of holes made to take screws with a countersunk head. Unless you recess the hole, no matter how tightly you drive the screw home, the head will never lie absolutely flush with the surface. If you are likely to be drilling holes in metal and want to countersink them in the same way, you will have to buy a special countersink bit specially hardened and ground to cut metal. Don't try to use your woodwork bit for the job or you will spoil it.

For drilling metal you will need one final item—a steel centre punch. This tool is simply a short length of steel rod with a hardened and ground point. You place the point at the exact centre of the hole you want to drill in the metal and give it a sharp tap with a hammer. This makes a tiny depression which locates the point of the drill and stops it from sliding about when you switch it on.

FITTING THE DRILL IN THE CHUCK
Most practical people will not need to be told how to put a drill in a chuck, but as everybody has to do it for the first time, if you haven't done it before, this is the way:

Look at the chuck on your drill and you will see that it has a bright steel collar with teeth around the front and when this toothed ring is turned with the chuck key it grips the drill tight between the three jaws sticking out at the front end of the chuck. If you grasp the toothed ring you will find that it turns easily and as it does so the three jaws open or close depending on which way you turn the ring. This is the quickest way to start adjusting the chuck to hold the shank of the drill; you only need the key for the final tightening up or for releasing the jaws when you want to remove the drill.

So, to fit a drill in the chuck, you first make sure the power tool is switched off at the mains plug, turn the chuck ring with your fingers until you can insert the drill between the jaws, push the drill shank in as far as it will go and then tighten the jaws once more by hand. Make sure that the drill shank is actually in the centre of the three jaws; if you are not careful, particularly when you are fitting drills as small as 1/32 in. or 1/16 in. you can easily grip the drill off centre between two of the jaws. Then, when you start up the drill, it will probably break or run wild and damage the surface of the work.

Once you are satisfied that the drill is correctly held in the chuck, you insert the chuck key spindle in one of the three holes around the collar just in front of the toothed ring and turn it clockwise until the drill is gripped tight in the jaws. The teeth around the chuck key fit into those on the chuck ring and as you turn the key it screws up the collar much tighter than if you simply tightened the ring by hand. When you've tightened the key in the first hole repeat the operation for each of the two remaining holes. (If you wonder why

The right way to fit a drill in the chuck. The key must be tightened in all three holes. Make sure that small drills-1/16 in. and 1/32 in.-are gripped centrally by all three jaws.

you should switch off the power at the mains plug before you fit the drill, just think what would happen if you accidentally pressed the on-off trigger while you were tightening the chuck key!)

HOLES IN WOOD
You are now ready to practise drilling holes and the best thing to start on is a piece of scrap wood such as a bit of 1 in. thick board held in the vice or clamped down on the edge of a table or work bench so that the drill will be clear of the surface when it comes out at the other side. Mark the spot where you want to drill the hole and make a depression to locate the drill with a centre punch or point of a nail.

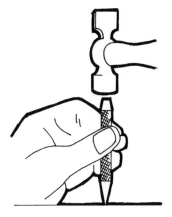

Before starting to drill a hole you make a small depression with a pointed punch to locate the drill in the centre of the hole and prevent it from slipping.

Now switch on the power at the mains plug and check that your power drill is ready for work by quickly pressing and releasing the trigger in the front of the tool handle; the motor will start and stop as you do so. Now locate the point of the drill in the depression left by the punch and check that you are holding the tool so that the drill is at right angles to the surface whether you look at it from the side or front. You won't find this easy at first so, if you can, get a helper with a good eye for straightness to stand a few feet away and check the angle. (Drilling square on to the job is taken care of automatically if the power tool is mounted in the Black & Decker

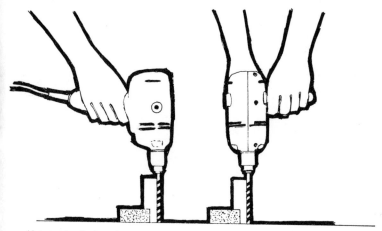

Always check that the drill is at right angles to the surface whether looked at from front or side. Novices should use a small engineer's square as illustrated or mount the power tool in a vertical drill stand.

vertical drill stand [p 101], but in any case it is worth-while persevering until you can hold the drill square on to the job without any outside help.)

Now, with the drill point located and the drill at right angles to the surface, press the trigger switch and hold the tool steady while the drill runs into the wood. Put just enough pressure on the drill to keep it cutting into the wood. If you hear the motor slowing down you are over-loading it. This may be because you are forcing it to cut too fast or because the drill chips are not being cleared by the flutes in the drill and are packing tight inside the hole and acting as a brake. The solution is to withdraw the drill from the hole when you hear the motor slowing down and clear the drill flutes before you start drilling again.

The critical part of the operation comes when the point of the drill is about to break out at the other side of the piece of timber. Once the point cuts its way out, instead of pressing on the tool you have to be ready to hold it back. If you are not on the lookout for the sudden change, the nose of the drill will slice fiercely into the ring of wood still remaining around the back edge of the hole and pull itself through it with a jerk that will probably tear away the wood fibres around the hole and leave a nasty ragged edge. Or it may try to bite off more than it can chew and stall the motor. What

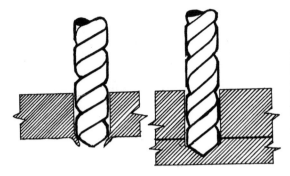

When the point of the drill passes through the material it tends to tear it and leave a ragged hole. You can prevent this by backing the material with a piece of scrap wood.

happens is that once the nose of the drill breaks through the wood, the spiral flutes act like a corkscrew and pull the drill through the break right up to the end of the flutes and at that point the drill can even jam and stop turning.

If you keep a firm grip on the tool and let the drill feed very slowly forward as it breaks through, you can prevent it from stalling but you will still get a ragged hole because the last bits of wood simply splinter and get pushed out of the way of the drill instead of being cut away cleanly. There may be jobs where this won't worry you, but mostly you will want to leave a clean sharp edge to the hole. You can make sure of this by taking just a little trouble.

One way of stopping the wood from splintering is to clamp a piece of scrap board to the back of the piece you are drilling. You then run the drill right through into the scrap. Another way is to drill a small diameter pilot hole—say 1/8 in. diameter—right through your work piece. Next run the full size drill half way through the board from one side and then turn the board over and finish the hole from the other side, using the pilot hole to guide your main drill each time. This way any splintering takes place in the middle of the hole and gets smoothed out as the drill runs through.

So long as you use the highest speed you are not likely to have any trouble with small diameter drills but an ordinary power tool is not powerful enough to drill a big diameter hole of 1/2 in. to 1 in. fast enough to prevent it splintering. In any case, if you are using a big diameter drill—anything over 3/8 in.—it is worth while drilling a pilot hole through first to guide the main drill.

Another way of preventing the drill from tearing the hole. Left and centre: Drill part of the way from one side and complete the hole by drilling from the opposite side. Any tearing will occur in the meeting place, out of sight. Right: It helps if you drill a small pilot hole right through first.

HOLES IN METAL

Now you know the way to use your power tool to drill plain everyday holes in wood you are ready to tackle holes in metal. For your first attempts use a piece of scrap metal—preferably steel, about 1/4 in. thick that you can hold firmly in a vice. Drilling holes in thin metal is a little tricky so make sure you have a thick enough piece of scrap when you start. (Holes in thin sheet metal come later.)

First mark the position of the hole by scratching a cross on the surface with a sharp point. Then place the point of your centre punch where the two scratches cross and give the punch a sharp tap with the hammer. This should leave a depression deep enough to locate the point of the drill.

Next fit a 3/16 in. drill in the chuck and tighten it up, using the chuck key in each of the three holes in the nose of the chuck in turn. 3/16 in. or thereabouts is a good size for practice; as a beginner you are more apt to break a smaller drill while larger sizes are best tackled when you have learned how to deal with the point of break-through.

Start by putting a few drops of ordinary lubricating oil on the centre punch mark, then locate the point of the drill in it and set the drill square on to the job exactly as you did for drilling wood. While you maintain a steady pressure on the tool, press the trigger switch. As the drill goes into action, maintain just enough pressure to keep it cutting as shown by the small chips or spirals of metal (swarf) being pushed out. You will hear the note of the motor drop a little as you do this, but it should still be turning quite fast. Don't press on so hard that the note drops to a low grunting noise. That means overloading and trouble. On the other hand don't ease off the pressure so much that the drill just rubs the metal without cutting. This is bad because it heats up and blunts the cutting edges of the drill and on some metals it may also produce a hard polished glaze. This glaze can be very difficult to bite through without putting excessive pressure behind the drill.

From time to time, withdraw the drill from the hole, clear away the swarf and drop in another spot of oil before you start drilling again. Presently the point of the drill will start to come through at the other side of the piece of metal and this is the critical moment when you have to keep a firm hold on the tool to stop it from jumping forward and jamming as the cutting edges of the drill bite deeply into the last of the metal at the bottom of the hole. The knack will come with practice, but at first you may even find it impossible to stop the drill from 'cork-screwing' through the jagged opening at the bottom of the hole. When this happens the quickest way of cleaning up the end of the hole is to fit a metal-cutting countersink bit in the chuck, insert the point of the bit in the hole from the other side and press the switch. The countersink bit will clean up the hole in a second or two, leaving the edge slightly bevelled which in most cases is an advantage anyway.

When drilling metal, ease off the pressure and hold the drill firmly as the point starts to break through or it may 'corkscrew' out at the other side and stall the power tool.

Drilling large holes is easier if you make a small pilot hole first. The pilot drill should be equal in diameter to the thickness of the chisel point of the large drill.

You can avoid breakthrough troubles with metal in the same way as you do with wood—i.e. you can back up the piece you want to drill with another piece of scrap and take the drill right through both, or you can clear the way with a small diameter pilot drill and then drill half of the main hole from one side and half from the other.

(A pilot hole is always worth while when you want to drill a large diameter hole in either wood or metal, first because it is the centre of the big drill point that takes most of the power to push through and second because there is nothing to keep the big drill in the true centre of the hole until the conical point has drilled below the surface and the drill gets its shoulders into the actual hole.)

You can drill holes in metal up to the full diameter of the drill chuck even with a single speed power drill, but if you have a 2-speed drill it makes things a lot easier—and your drills will stay sharp longer—if you use the slow speed for holes in metal over 1/4 in. diameter. You would, of course, drill the pilot hole at the high speed.

GETTING BACK TO CENTRE

If you drill a large hole without first locating it accurately with a small pilot hole, the drill is always apt to wander before it has the sides of the hole to guide it. Normally you will not know if the point of the drill has wandered off beam because the centre punch hole marking the accurate position will have been drilled away. However, if you first mark the outline of the hole on the surface you can always tell if the drill is running astray.

On wood you can draw the hole with a pencil in a pair of compasses. You can do the same thing on a metal surface if you first whiten it with chalk. But remember, the oil you use to lubricate the point of the drill will blot out the pencil mark so with the same centre punch as you used for marking the centre of the hole you need to make light punch marks around the circle drawn on the chalked surface. Four punch marks—at '12, 3, 6 and 9 o'clock'—are all you need.

When you have marked out the centre and circumference of the hole in this way, you start drilling, but this time you stop before the point of the drill has drilled out to its full diameter. Now look at the circle left by the point of the drill and compare it with the one marking the true position of the hole you want to drill (or the centre punch holes on a metal surface).

How to get back to centre:
(a) Circumference of hole marked on face of metal to be drilled.

(b) Drill has made a bad start and is running off centre.

(c) Groove cut in side of crater with cold chisel.

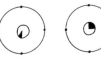

(d) Drill cuts towards groove and runs back to centre.

(e) Full diameter of drill now engaged; walls of hole prevent drill from wandering off again.

If the drilled out core is concentric with the marked hole you can carry on with the drilling operation, but if it lies seriously off centre you will have to rectify the error before drilling any further. If the error is small you can correct it by using the centre punch. To do this, place the point of the punch in the centre of the drill crater, slant the punch so that it points towards the true centre and give it a few taps with the hammer. Now drill a little further and again check the position of the two circles. You may have to do this more than once before the drill gets back to its proper position.

If the error is too big to be corrected this way, you can make a big shift by cutting a groove in the drill crater down the side to which you want the drill to move. In wood you can chip a suitable groove out with the edge of a chisel. In metal you can either make a row of deep punch marks or cut out a groove with the nose of a diamond-point cold chisel.

HOLES IN VERY THIN SHEET METAL

There are no problems in drilling small holes in thin sheet material, the trouble comes when you want to make holes from around 3/16 in. diameter upwards. When the drill is big in relation to the thickness of the sheet, the point comes through the back before the shoulders of the drill enter the metal and have a hole to support them. With nothing to locate it either in the centre or round the edges, the drill can run completely out of control and tear its way through leaving behind anything but the neat clean cut circle you hoped to see.

It will help a lot if you back up the sheet with a piece of hard scrap wood. This will keep the drill centred after the point passes through the sheet, but if the metal you are drilling is thin or soft—like sheet aluminium or copper—the cutting edges of the drill can still tear into it and lift it away from the backing material. The answer is to clamp the sheet tightly between two pieces of board so that the drill cuts through a sandwich with the metal held firmly in the centre. This type of drilling operation is much easier if you have the power drill mounted in a vertical drill stand (p 101).

Always make a point of clamping sheet metal firmly to the top of the bench before you attempt to drill it. Never risk holding it with your hand, even when drilling small holes because if the drill jams it can pull the sheet out of your fingers and spin it around before you can get your hand out of the way.

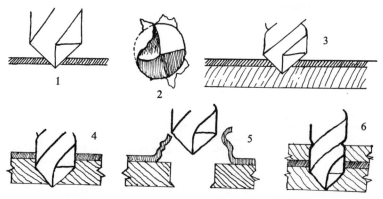

1 & 2, when point of drill penetrates sheet before shoulders are supported by hole, it tears instead of cutting. 3 & 4, thick sheet metal can be backed with scrap wood to give a clean hole. 5, thin sheet metal may lift off and tear even when backed up. 6, the answer is to sandwich the sheet between two pieces of scrap wood.

Even with the metal sandwiched between two pieces of board it pays to open out the hole gradually, with several pilot holes increasing the diameter in steps. For instance, to drill a 1/2 in. diameter hole in thin metal, you might start with a 1/8 in. drill and follow up with 1/4 in., 3/8 in., 7/16 in. and finally, 1/2 in.

However careful you are you cannot avoid finishing with a raised burr of metal around the hole where the drill has pushed through. You should always remove this burr as it is dangerously sharp, and it can also be troublesome if it gets bent back into the hole. The quickest way to deal with it is to cut it away with a few turns of a countersink bit or a large diameter drill mounted in your power tool.

For bigger holes still, the answer is to use a holesaw preferably with the power drill mounted in a vertical drill stand (p 101). A holesaw is a metal drum with a toothed rim which cuts a circular hole in the same way as a metal cutting hacksaw blade. The drum is held on the shank of a twist drill by a screw through the central boss. You fix the stem of the twist drill in the power tool chuck in the usual way and adjust the position of the saw drum so that the nose of the twist-drill sticks out beyond the teeth. If possible you clamp the sheet metal you are going to drill on to a support of scrap wood and drill a hole right through in the normal way with the twist drill. You then advance the edge of the saw until it makes contact with the sheet metal, and continue to exert sufficient pressure to keep it cutting but not enough to overload the motor. The twist drill keeps the saw running true until it cuts clear through the metal, leaving a clean, accurate hole. With this cutting tool there are no breakthrough problems and you can even saw out a hole in a tank where you cannot support the metal from the back. Good holesaws are designed so that the cut out disc is retained in the saw and you have to lever it out with a pointed tool. This is to prevent it from falling into the tank and being difficult to recover.

You can buy holesaws of this type singly or in sets ranging from 1/2 in. diameter to as large as 4 in. While all these sizes will fit a 1/4 in. power drill chuck it is not advisable to cut sheet steel, e.g. a metal water tank, with anything bigger than a 1 1/4 in. holesaw with the normal single speed drill. Over that diameter you should use either the low speed of a 2-speed drill (1 3/4 in. to 2 in. diameter) or a speed reducing gearbox (2 in. to 4 in. diameter).

The thickness of the sheet that you can cut with a holesaw of this type is never more than about 3/16 in. because of its construction. If you are drilling a number of holes with a holesaw, you have to remember to remove the disc of metal retained inside the drum from the previous hole before you start a new one. As a general rule, any material that can be cut with a hacksaw can be cut with a holesaw. To lubricate the saw, use light oil for steel and paraffin for aluminium and its alloys.

Larger holes in sheet metal are best cut with a Black & Decker jigsaw, described in a later chapter.

Occasionally you may want to cut a large or irregular shape in a piece of metal too thick to tackle with a jigsaw. If you don't mind spending the time you can do the job with your Black & Decker power drill by drilling a row of holes almost touching each other along the outline of the piece you want to remove.

First chalk the surface of the metal and then draw the outline in pencil or mark the cutting line with a suitably coloured felt pen. Next, with a pair of dividers or a ruler tick the line about every 1/8 in. and mark it with a centre punch. Then, with a 1/8 in. twist drill in the power drill you drill a hole at every centre punch mark. If you want to speed up the job you can use a row of 1/4 in. holes. When you have gone all round the outline, join up all the holes by cutting away any metal between them with a thin flat chisel or sawing it out with a padsaw that you can buy for a small sum at any tool counter.

HOLES IN WOODWORK

Many of the holes you will want to drill will be to take the screws for joining two pieces of wood together. There is a right and a wrong way and most people tend naturally to do it the wrong way. The favourite way with beginners is to drill a hole in the top piece of wood just a bit smaller than the screw they are going to use. Then they pop the screw in the hole, put one piece of wood on top of the other and drive the screw home, leaving it to cut its own way into the lower piece. This way, no matter how hard they turn the screwdriver, the two pieces of wood never draw any closer and the head of the screw sticks out above the surface making a permanent hazard for hands or clothes.

To do the job the right way you need three drills, not just one. The first is the pilot drill, just a little smaller in diameter than the core diameter of the threaded part of the woodscrew. The second is the clearance drill, the same size as or slightly larger than the plain part of the woodscrew. The third is the countersink bit which is the same for all the woodscrews you are likely to use. If the thought of all this extra work worries you, take heart, you can buy a combination drill bit (p. 39) which does all three jobs at the same time. However, if you don't mind doing it the hard way, here is how you go about the job:

Wrong way to drill timber for wood-screw fastening. As the screw is already tight in the top plank, further tightening doesn't pull the joint any closer. And as the hole is not countersunk the head of the screw will always project above the surface.

The right way. First drill the pilot hole for the screw thread, then drill and countersink a clearance hole in the top plank. Tightening the screw closes the joint because the shank does not bind in the top plank. This time the screw head does not project above the surface.

1 Clamp the two pieces of wood together in their final position and punch the positions of all the screw holes with a blunt centre punch.

2 Fit the pilot drill in the chuck and mark the length of the screw on it with a piece of electrician's tape. (If you are going to drill a lot of holes to the same depth you can make a more reliable gauge by cutting a piece of dowelling or a cork to the correct length, running the drill down the centre and leaving it in position to act as a stop when the drill has reached the right depth.)

3 Drill all the marked holes right up to the tape on the drill.

4 Separate the two pieces of wood and with the clearance drill in the chuck, drill out all the holes in the top piece.

5 With the countersink bit in the chuck, countersink all the openings of the clearance holes so that when you insert a woodscrew the head lies flush with or slightly below the surface of the wood.

6 Clean off any splinters or sawdust from the mating faces of the two pieces of wood, place them together and insert all the woodscrews in the clearance holes.

7 Drive home all the woodscrews with the screwdriver, starting with the two farthest apart, then the one in the middle and so on.

When you do the job this way, the screws pull the two pieces of wood together as you tighten them down, making a tight joint, and the heads finish up looking neat and flush with the surface.

The following chart will help you to choose the correct size drill for both pilot and clearance holes for the sizes of wood screw most used by handymen.

Gauge of woodscrew	Size of pilot hole (in.) (Hard wood)	Size of pilot hole (in.) (Soft wood)	Size of clearance hole (in.)
4	5/64	1/16	1/8
6	5/64	1/16	5/32
8	3/32	5/64	3/16
10	1/8	7/64	7/32

You will see that you can use a smaller pilot drill for soft wood. The clearance hole, however, is the same for both kinds.

COMBINATION DRILL BITS

If you are likely to be doing a lot of woodwork fixing jobs you can simplify the whole operation by using a special type of drill bit which combines the pilot drill, clearance drill and countersink in a single tool. As the sizes of the three sections of the combination bit depend on the number of the screw and its length, you need a range of these bits to cover all the screws you may want to use. However, the drills are sold in sets, mounted on a card with full instructions so that you can select the right bit for the job in hand.

Many of these sets of drills have an adjustable depth guide which lets you select one of three countersink depths. The first position leaves the screw head flush with the surface. The second sinks it slightly below the surface so that you can fill in with putty before painting. The third setting leaves a deeper recess to take a dowel cut from the same timber. The last is the one to use when you want to leave the natural wood grain to show instead of covering it with paint.

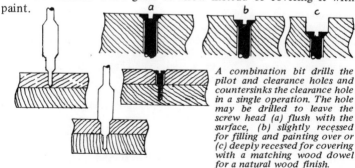

A combination bit drills the pilot and clearance holes and countersinks the clearance hole in a single operation. The hole may be drilled to leave the screw head (a) flush with the surface, (b) slightly recessed for filling and painting over or (c) deeply recessed for covering with a matching wood dowel for a natural wood finish.

Of all the jobs around the home that call for a power tool the commonest is probably the need for fastening things to walls inside and outside the house—shelves, cupboards, hooks, electric light fittings, heaters and all the other fixtures that add to our comfort and convenience. And this is a job that must be done properly because most of the things you fix to a wall can cause expense or injury if they break away and crash to the floor. Unfortunately walls are not designed to make the job easy. Mostly you have to deal with a plastered brick wall. This is usually about 1/2 in. of plaster (which may be as hard as flint or as crumbly as a fruit cake) over bricks (hard or soft) with mortar joints (hard, soft or often just empty gaps).

In the bad old days the only way to get a firm fixing in this sort of surface was to batter a hole through the plaster and brickwork with a heavy hammer and chisel and then plug the resulting hole with a wedge of hard wood that would hold a long woodscrew or a large ugly nail. Finally you replastered the wall around the fixing and often had to make good cracked plaster on the other side of the shattered wall.

Nowadays the whole process has been civilised by the tungsten carbide tipped masonry drill. These drills will cut quite happily through the toughest brickwork and although they lose their edge in time they can be resharpened. Tungsten carbide is too hard to be ground on an ordinary carborundum wheel or grindstone; these drills must be sharpened on a special diamond impregnated or silicon carbide grinding wheel. Some tool stores have the special type of wheel and offer a quick, on-the-spot resharpening service. Otherwise you can return the drill to the manufacturer and have it resharpened. Either way the cost is very much less than you would pay for a new drill. These drills will make a clean, accurate hole which will accept a suitable size of Rawlplug or similar fixing device designed to provide a secure, self-locking anchorage for your woodscrew.

You will get the most reliable fixing if you can drill your hole into the body of the brick. The 1/2 in. or so of mortar between the bricks may or may not be sound just where you want to drill. Generally whatever you want to screw to the wall will cover a big enough area to hide a pilot hole or two. So use a small diameter masonry drill and make a test hole at the spot where you want to fix the screw. The drill will run quickly through the plaster rendering and with any luck you will feel it slow down as it reaches the face of a brick.

If you are unlucky and hit a gap between bricks, the drill will run straight through the mortar without slowing, in which case you will have to make another trial hole. Make the next hole 1/2 in. above or below the old hole and if you struck a horizontal joint the first time you have a better chance of hitting solid brick with your next shot. However, if your first hole went into a vertical joint then you may still go into the same joint again after the move up or down so you will have to make another trial 1/2 in. to the right or left.

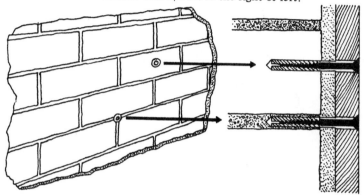

Wall fixtures are firmest when the screw holes are in the brick (top) and not in the mortar (bottom). If in doubt make test holes with a small drill to locate the middle of the brick.

If you find you are still in mortar with your third hole, then you have been working around the corner of a brick and you only have to move 1/2 in. up from your last hole to be certain of landing in solid brick at last. (You may hit brick at your first shot; you have to be very unlucky indeed to have to drill three useless holes before you find a brick. However, at the worst the whole operation takes only a few seconds and it will leave you with three 1/8 in. holes at the corners of a 1 in. square to plug, or hide. Of course if your fixture isn't going to be big enough to cover your misses then you will just have to settle for the hole in the mortar if your drill went into a gap first time. In that case you should use the largest diameter masonry drill and plug in your kit and a screw long enough to allow for the thickness of your fixture and at least two inches in the wall.)

Once you are sure that your drill will go into a brick, decide what gauge of screw you are going to use—usually 8, 10 or 12. Next fix the length of the screw, taking the thickness of the fixture—batten, wall bracket etc.—and adding 1/2 in. for the plaster rendering and 1 in to go into the brickwork.

To complete the job you will need the following:

(a) The right diameter and length of masonry drill to suit the screw. (The Black & Decker masonry drills are stamped with the screw gauge 8, 10 or 12.)

(b) A fixing plug to suit the screw. (You will find the size marked on the plug pack.) The length of the plug should equal the length of the threaded part of the screw.

(c) If you are screwing a wooden batten or board to the wall you will also need a clearance drill for the screw hole in the wood and a countersink.

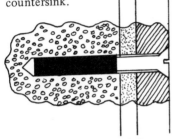

Correct: The plug is only as long as the threaded portion of the screw and is pushed clear of the batten and plaster rendering.

The procedure is as follows:

1 Drill· the screw hole in the board, batten or other wood fixture with the clearance drill and countersink the hole.

2 Fit the masonry drill in the chuck and if yours is a 2-speed drill, engage the slow speed.

3 Mark the depth of the hole on the drill with a slip of electrician's tape.

4 Start drilling at the marked spot, making sure that the drill is square on to the surface of the wall.

5 Maintain a constant pressure on the drill to keep it cutting steadily.

6 Once the drill starts cutting into the brickwork withdraw it from time to time and clear the dust from the hole to prevent jamming.

7 Stop drilling when you reach the marked depth, blow the hole clear of dust (keeping your eyes closed) and insert the fixing plug, pushing it flush with the wall surface.

8 Rub a smear of soap or washing up liquid on the screw, pass it through the countersunk hole in the fixture and start the point in the hole in the plug.

9 Tap the screw gently and it will push the plug down to the end of the hole in the brick.

10 Drive the screw home to pull the fixture tight against the surface of the wall.

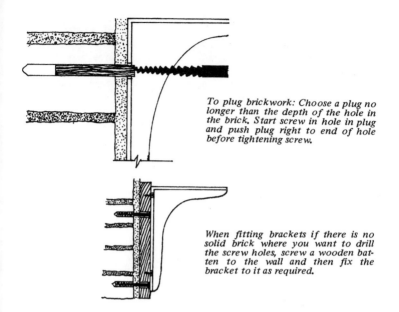

To plug brickwork: Choose a plug no longer than the depth of the hole in the brick. Start screw in hole in plug and push plug right to end of hole before tightening screw.

When fitting brackets if there is no solid brick where you want to drill the screw holes, screw a wooden batten to the wall and then fix the bracket to it as required.

If the fixture is not likely to carry a heavy load you can settle for a hole in the mortar joint, otherwise it pays to go to the extra trouble to find a solid brick. However, once you have done that it will help you to drill other holes above or below if you remember that brick courses are usually laid either 4 bricks to 1 ft or 7 bricks to 2 ft.

With some of the fixtures you may want to screw to the wall, the screw holes are already there, e.g. in the usual type of metal bracket to support shelves, wall cupboards and so on. With this type of fitting you have to put up with whatever your drill finds, brick, mortar or thin air. The best way to deal with this situation is to fasten a wooden batten to the wall first and then screw the fitting on to the batten. Of course you can always try without a batten and then if your drill runs into soft spots (or runs off the mark so that you can't fix the fitting upright) you can fit a batten covering the unsightly evidence and mount your fixture on that in the usual way.

HOLES IN PARTITION WALLS

When you are fixing to outside walls you will usually be drilling into brickwork or concrete, but internal walls, especially nowadays, are usually made of lighter and cheaper materials since they have no great loads to carry. New materials and an increasing range of manufactured hardboards are continually being introduced for this type of partitioning in addition to the commoner breeze blocks, aerated concrete and plasterboard.

However, all these materials are softer than ordinary masonry and there is nothing difficult about drilling the holes with a power tool (which is what this part of the book is about). The difficulty is simply one of getting a fixing to hold in the hole you have drilled.

If you want a screw fixing to hold in a hollow wall faced with hard board, you would usually use a special fastening which pushes through the hole and then expands at the back of the board as you drive the screw home. Another type of fastener has a pivoted section which turns to form a bridge across the back of the hole once you have pushed it through into the cavity. Finally, for getting a screwhold in soft or crumbling materials you can buy a number of proprietary fillers which you press into the hole where they adhere to the material and set hard so that you can drive a screw into them. With some of these fillers you press the woodscrew into the mastic before setting takes place. When the filler hardens it stays permanently moulded to the shape of the thread, allowing the screw to be removed and replaced without affecting its grip in the wall surface.

HOLES IN CONCRETE

Concrete is usually a mixture of cement, sand and gravel. The cement and sand present no problems to the ordinary masonry drill, but gravel may contain pebbles which are extremely hard and almost impossible to cut even with a tungsten carbide tipped drill. If you try drilling a hole in concrete, e.g. the lintel of a door or window,

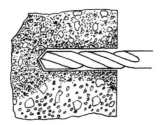

Concrete includes hard flinty aggregate which soon blunts even masonry drills. A rotary hammer drill or attachment gets over this obstacle by breaking up the aggregate with thousands of impacts per minute as it rotates. For this type of drilling you need a special percussion drill.

with an ordinary masonry drill, you may get along fine for a while and then the drill will suddenly stop moving forward. If you press harder the point of the drill will probably squeal in protest but nothing useful will happen. Keep up the pressure and you will simply overheat the drill and dull the edge; or the drill may work off to the side to by-pass the trouble and the hole will have a slant.

The answer is to break up the flint obstacle and there are two ways of doing it. One is to withdraw the drill and clear the way with a hammer and a hand tool—e.g. a Rawltool. This operation is effective but slow and if you are not an expert at handling a hammer and chisel you can easily end up with skinned knuckles.

The other way is to use one of the Black & Decker 2-speed hammer drills. These are normal 2-speed models with the addition of a high frequency hammer action. This action reproduces the combined turning and hammering action of the hand held type of tool but at a very much faster rate; in fact it delivers over 20,000 blows per minute, causing even the hardest material to crumble away. As well as having a much higher rate of penetration into masonry than the hand tool, the hammer drill does with thousands of light taps what the hand tool tries to do in single heavy blows which always involve the risk of cracking the surrounding masonry.

To engage the rotary hammer action you lift up a ring between the body of the drill and the chuck, turn it through 90 degrees and let it go again. You can use the hammer action in either low or high gear: at the fast speed you will get through the work quicker but the drill will not stay sharp for as long; at the slow speed you will get there just the same in the end and your drill will not need sharpening so often.

If you are still wondering what sort of power drill to buy and you are likely to be doing a lot of drilling in concrete, the answer is certainly a hammer drill. On the other hand, if you already have a power drill, then the answer could be a Black & Decker rotary hammer attachment (p 181).

HOLES IN GLAZED TILES

When you are mounting fixtures on glazed tiles in the kitchen or bathroom you can do the job with your power drill and an ordinary tipped masonry drill. But you need to take a lot of care in starting the hole. With a centre punch you run the risk of cracking the tile. The way to do it is to fit your smallest masonry drill in the chuck, rest the point on the tile where you want to drill the hole and turn the chuck backwards and forwards with your hand until you feel the glaze crumble. Once you have penetrated the glaze you can go ahead and drill the hole in the normal way for masonry. You may find it even easier to start the drill by sticking a piece of 'Sellotape' tape on the surface of the tile first and drilling through it. The tape will prevent the point of the drill from skidding about on the glazed surface.

HOLES IN GLASS
This is a job calling for some skill, so practise on odd pieces that don't matter before you tackle anything you care about. A normal drill or even a masonry drill bit is useless for glass; you need to buy a special glass-cutting bit, and as the drilling must be done at a slow speed you can only do it if you have a 2-speed or variable speed model or, better still, a hand wheel brace. And while you can do it with the power drill held in your hand, you'll be much safer with it held in the vertical drill stand.

For drilling glass you need to keep the bit constantly supplied with lubricant. Turpentine is best but you have to use plain water for mirrors as turpentine might dissolve the backing.

For holes in glass use a tipped drill made specially for the job. Build a ring of putty around the hole to hold a pool of turpentine for lubricating the drill point.

First make sure that your sheet of glass is resting on a firm level surface and check particularly that it is in contact immediately behind the hole. If you are using a vertical drill stand you will have to position and secure the glass and its support so that the point of the drill bit comes down at the right spot. Then proceed like this:
1 Build a little ring of stiff putty on the surface of the glass around the position where you require the hole and pour some turpentine into it.
2 Bring the point of the bit into contact with the glass and turn the chuck backwards and forwards to break the skin and start the hole.

3 With the drill running at its slowest speed, press it gently on to the surface of the glass. Lift the bit out of the hole from time to time to help the lubricant to circulate.

4 As soon as the tip of the bit breaks through the other side of the glass, turn the glass over, position everything accurately so that the bit is central with the hole and start drilling again, being specially careful to control the speed. (This time you will have to keep 'swabbing' the drill with a soft brush dipped in lubricant.)

5 Finally take the razor-sharp edges off the hole by rubbing with a piece of fine emery cloth wrapped round a pencil and wetted with turpentine.

If you are working on a vertical surface you will not be able to build a pool of lubricant for the drill point. In this case you will have to keep swabbing lubricant on the drill point with a soft brush. It also helps to roll a strip of absorbent cloth around the drill to soak up the lubricant and feed it to the drill point.

You can also drill holes in glass with a short length of copper tube of the correct diameter in place of the drill. The cutting medium is a thin paste made by mixing emery powder or silicon carbide 220 grit with turpentine. The particles of grit become embedded in the soft copper and turn the tube into a hollow drill. You have to keep raising the tube from time to time to allow fresh particles to replace the worn ones and allow the turpentine to circulate and prevent overheating. To get a clean edge when the drill breaks through, the glass you are drilling should be backed up by a piece of scrap glass plate in close contact with it.

CHOOSING A POWER TOOL TO SUIT YOUR REQUIREMENTS

Up to this point we have been talking about power drills as drills and nothing else. You now know what sorts there are and what jobs you can do with them. At the back of the book you will find detailed information on each separate Black & Decker model. The range covers models with chuck sizes from 5/16 in. up to 1/2 in. single speed, 2-speed and variable speed and finally 2-speed hammer drills.

The most expensive model costs around three times as much as the cheapest model, so which is the best one for you to buy? If you only want a power drill the answer would depend simply on how much and what sort of drilling you think you're likely to be doing. There is no point in buying a model to cut 1/2 in. holes in steel if you never want to do more than home carpentry. Even the cheapest and smallest single speed power drill in the range is all you would need for drilling screw holes up to 1/4 in. diameter in wood. The much more expensive 1/2 in. model would not do the job any better, so you would not get any extra value for the additional cost.

However, once you think of your power drill in terms of the attachments, the picture changes. If you expect to be doing a lot of circular sawing, jigsawing, wood turning or other jobs apart from drilling, then a more powerful and expensive model would probably serve you better and give you better value for money. Of course, even the smallest Black & Decker power drills are designed to take the full range of attachments, just as a Mini can tow a 4-berth caravan. Everything depends on how much use you intend to make of the extra power and facilities. If you are going to be using the saw almost constantly, it would probably be a better bargain to buy a simple power drill and an independent self-powered circular saw, rather than a powerful model drill with the circular saw attachment. You could buy the two independent tools for roughly the same amount as a comparable drill and circular saw attachment.

The next chapters deal with the various integral Black & Decker tools one by one and in each case, immediately following the description of the drill attachment, you can read about the self-powered tool designed to do the same job. Then you can make up your mind which equipment will be the best buy for your particular work programme.

Note: The statement that all Black & Decker attachments will fit all Black & Decker home user power tools does not apply to the model D900 which was intended for use as a drill only. This model has now been discontinued and has therefore not been included in the book. Anything said about the use of attachments should be regarded as applying to all current Black & Decker home user power drills except the D900.

CIRCULAR SAWS

A power driven circular saw is one of the most useful pieces of workshop equipment that anyone can buy. It probably saves more time and effort than any other power tool on the market. You may think that you do so little wood sawing that you can manage very well with a rusty old handsaw hanging up in the wood shed. But when you add the sweat of even the little bit of handsawing you do to the cost of the jobs you pay to get done because you do not possess a decent power saw, the answer will probably surprise you into rushing out and buying one.

You can buy a circular saw attachment for your power drill for a few pounds—not much more than you would pay for hand saws that would do the same work but take ten times as long. This particular attachment will do a surprisingly good job or you can buy an integral tool for a few extra pounds if you have a lot of sawing to do and you do not want to waste time changing over tools.

A circular saw has teeth like an ordinary hand saw but they are cut around a circular steel blade instead of along a straight one. So a circular saw goes on cutting while a straight saw wastes time and effort in pulling back to the start again at the end of every stroke.

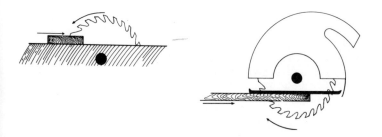

Left: Bench mounted circular saws turn so that the sawing action presses the wood down on to the bench. Right: Portable circular saws turn in the opposite direction to press the wood up against the shoe.

The wood has to be held against the thrust of the teeth or they could not cut it. On a bench saw the cutting action of the teeth is from the top downwards and the bench provides the support. With a portable saw, however, the saw works above the surface of the wood you are cutting so the teeth cut from below upwards and the wood is supported by the shoe of the saw and not by the work bench. (If the portable saw blade teeth cut downwards the cutting action would simply lift it off the surface and the saw would jump about instead of doing its job. It is as well to know this at the start so that you will not think the teeth are facing the wrong way in the illustrations and you will be in no danger of fitting the blade the wrong way round in your own power saw.)

As in most other saws the teeth are bent outwards or 'set' so that they make a cut slightly wider than the blade. This gets rid of friction between the blade and the sides of the cut and makes sawing easier and quicker.

The diameter of the saw blades gives you a good guide to the performance, power and price of a portable saw because a bigger blade will cut thicker wood, require a more powerful motor and stronger construction and so cost more.

A portable circular saw, like the power drill, relies for its terrific performance on a small high speed electric motor geared down to the cutting speed of the tool by a built-in gearbox. In this case the speed of the motor may be 20,000 r.p.m. or more while the saw will be turning at around 2–3,000 r.p.m. depending on the diameter of the blade (a 5 in. circular saw blade, gives a peripheral speed of around 2–3000 ft per min., which is satisfactory for the kind of wood sawing done by the normal home user.)

The tool rests on a shoe with a slit in it for the saw blade. The distance the saw blade projects below the shoe controls the depth of the cut and so the thickness of the wood you can saw. The position of the shoe is adjustable so that you can alter the depth of cut. As a rule you set the depth so that the saw just runs out at the other side of the wood you are cutting; there is no point in having more of the blade projecting than you are actually using.

Another useful facility that you get on some, but not all, power saws is a tilting shoe that lets you cut at an angle. With this type of saw the shoe is mounted on a hinge and can be locked by hand with a wing nut to make the blade cut at any angle up to 45° or more. (Of course you have to remember that with the saw working at an angle, you cannot get as big a depth of cut–e.g. if the thickest board your saw can cut at 90° is 1 1/2 in. you will not be able to tackle anything thicker than 1 in. with the shoe set to 45°.)

If you own a power drill you can buy an attachment that will turn it into a circular saw or you can buy a powered circular saw as an integral tool with its own built in motor and gearbox. Some attachments have a driving spindle that you fix in the chuck of your drill. These will work with any electric drill. Others, like the Black & Decker attachment, are designed to fit a particular manufacturer's power drill. The Black & Decker attachment fits in place of the chuck and the whole arrangement is thereby made more compact and easier to handle. The circular saw attachment and the circular saws in the Black & Decker range for the home user are typical of this class of power tool. The wide variety of Black & Decker industrial saws is outside the scope of this book, but the makers will always be pleased to send you information on these tools if you need a more powerful type of portable saw for continuous heavy duty.

THE BLACK & DECKER PORTABLE SAW ATTACHMENT

A portable saw attachment turns your power drill into a circular saw. Some attachments have a drive spindle that you simply grip in the chuck. You can use these with any type of power drill but they make a rather long and awkward assembly to handle. You get a more compact and handy saw when the attachment is designed to take the place of the chuck and fasten on to the actual case of the power tool. This is the principle of the Black & Decker portable saw attachment. It is specifically designed for the Black & Decker range of home user power tools so whichever model you own or intend to buy, you know that it will take the portable saw attachment.

The attachment has a fixed upper guard to the blade and a pivoted lower guard which automatically retracts to let the saw advance into the wood. The shoe has adjustments for both depth and sawing angle allowing a maximum depth of 1 1/4 in. or 7/8 in. when sawing at the maximum angle of 45°

The saw is fastened to the drive spindle of the drill by a bolt which also forms a pivot for the lower guard and the whole assembly is firmly attached to the case of the drill by a hinged clamp with claws which fit into the front ventilation slots in the front of the drill casing on all models. The clamp incorporates the saw handle and a single wing nut tightens it and holds the attachment firmly in place.

The lower guard rides loosely on the saw spindle and when the saw is running the slight friction tends to turn the guard with it. A stop arrests the movement of the guard when it reaches the fully closed position and holds it there until contact with the wood being sawn pushes it back just far enough to allow the saw to cut.

The attachment is also fitted with a detachable rip fence which can be used on either the right or the left of the shoe, giving a maximum sawing width of 3 1/2 in. on the right and 6 1/2 in. on the left.

The Black & Decker portable saw attachment turns any Black & Decker home user power tool into a portable circular saw with a full range of adjustments.

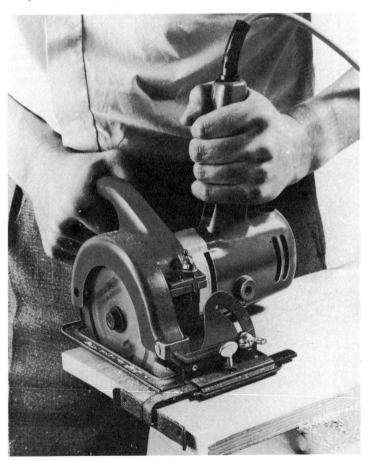

HOW TO USE THE ATTACHMENT

A word of warning: The drill trigger switch has a lock-on button and you may be tempted to use it on long cuts. This could be dangerous if the saw should slip out of your hand. So never lock the switch on when you are using the attachment as a portable saw. And always press the switch trigger once before plugging in to the mains; somebody may have locked it on with the button since you last used the tool.

Hold the attachment with your left hand on the pistol grip of the drill (which is now pointing up) and your right hand on the handle of the attachment.

Start by practising freehand sawing on a piece of scrap timber. It needs to be at least 18 in. long and 6 in. wide to offer a big enough surface for the shoe to rest on for the whole length of your trial saw cuts. Once you get the feel of the tool you'll be able to cut smaller pieces. And if you practise on old pieces of wood, make sure they are free from broken-off screws or nails.

Clamp the wood firmly to the bench with the bit you are going to saw through projecting over the edge. Now rule a thick black pencil line about 1/2 in. from the edge of the wood. You need to practise sawing along each side of the line until you can produce a straight cut that just touches the line. But before you start you will have to adjust the depth of the cut and the angle of the saw blade. Before making these adjustments be sure to pull the plug out of the mains supply socket—it is not enough to switch off at the socket, the tool should be disconnected altogether.

SETTING THE ANGLE OF CUT
Start with the saw set to cut at 90° to the surface of the wood. To do this you slacken off the wing nut in the protractor slot and set the reference mark to 0° on the protractor scale.

SETTING THE DEPTH OF CUT
The saw should be set so that it just runs out on the underside of the wood by no more than the depth of the teeth. To do this you slacken off the wing nut on the vertical slider at the back of the attachment and swing the shoe up or down until the saw blade projects just the right amount through the slot in the shoe. The quickest way to do this is to retract the lower guard and set the depth of the blade against a piece of wood of the same thickness as the wood you are going to saw. Finally, tighten down the wing nut on the slider.

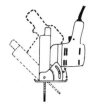

The body of the saw is pivoted so that the blade can be tilted to cut a bevel at any angle from -5° to +45°.

The body can also be swung up or down and locked in any position to set the depth of cut.

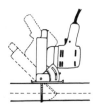

When you saw at an angle the maximum depth of cut is reduced.

SAWING FREEHAND

Release the rip fence locking screw and remove the fence. Now make a final check to see that all adjustments are firmly secured with the locking screws, that the saw blade is free to turn and the lower guard is working freely so that it turns to keep the exposed lower part of the blade covered when the saw is running.

1 Plug the lead into the mains socket.

2 Rest the front of the shoe plate on the wood with the saw blade clear of the edge and the guide notch lined up with the left-hand side of your pencil line.

3 Press the trigger switch to start the saw.

4 Slide the tool forward until the saw enters the wood and starts cutting.

5 Keep the shoe plate flat against the top of the wood and ease the saw forward. Don't press forward hard enough to slow the motor down seriously. The note should just fall slightly as the saw meets the wood. You will not saw any faster by forcing the pace; you are more likely to overload the motor and even damage it. (If the case feels hot after a long spell of sawing, let the motor run free for a while and the fan will soon cool it down.)

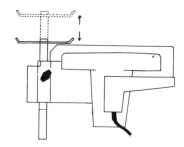

The front end of the shoe has a stepped guide to help you to saw freehand along a straight line. The steps indicate the sawing line (a) with the saw perpendicular and (b) with the saw at the maximum angle.

Sawing parallel to a straight edge is made easy by the adjustable rip fence.

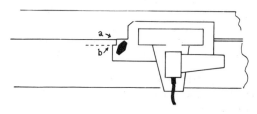

6 If the saw starts to run off the line, don't try to turn it back or you will twist the blade in the saw cut and the friction will overload the motor. The only cure is to draw the saw back to the place where it began to run off and then advance it slowly once more, along the correct line. So long as your error was on the waste side of the line, it won't matter, otherwise you will have to deal with the spoiled edge by planing it off or starting on a fresh piece of timber.

You will notice that the saw makes a gap slightly wider than the blade because the teeth are set off to each side to allow the rest of the blade to follow through without rubbing and wasting power. The gap, called the kerf, has to be allowed for when you are cutting timber to an exact size. The simplest way of allowing for the kerf is to mark your guide lines on the wood so that the dimensions will be right if the kerf just skims the waste wood side of the line.

SAWING AT AN ANGLE

With the angle adjustment you can set the saw blade so that it leaves the edge of the wood bevelled at any angle between 90° and a maximum slope of 45°. You simply slacken off the locking wing nut on the protractor scale, turn the shoe until the reference mark is opposite the angle you want and lock it once more with the screw. However, you are not ready to start sawing yet.

When you set the blade to cut at an angle you alter the depth of cut and the guide notch on the front of the shoe until it no longer lines up with the line of the saw cut. First you must re-set the depth of cut, lowering the saw until the teeth just clear the lower face of the work once more. For instance, suppose the depth was previously adjusted for a 90° cut with a 1 in. thick board. If you set the saw to cut at an angle of 45° you will have to increase the depth from just over 1 in. to almost 1 1/2 in. Perhaps this is beyond the capacity of your saw; if so you can always cut to the maximum depth and then clear away the remaining wood either with a handsaw or by turning the board over and setting your circular saw to make a second cut to join up with the first.

To provide a guide when sawing at an angle, the shoe has two guide notches or stops—one for use at 90° and the other, to one side of it, for cutting at 45°. To saw at any intermediate angle you can make a trial cut and then back out the saw and mark the position of the kerf with a pencil mark or scratch on the front of the shoe.

SAWING WITH THE RIP FENCE

When cutting wood you can either saw across the grain (cross cutting) or along the grain (ripping), and for this latter job a rip fence is very useful. (Special blades for these jobs are discussed on pages 68 to 69.)

If there is a straight side to the wood you are sawing and you want to cut a parallel sided strip off it, there is no need to mark out your cutting line beforehand. This is a job for the rip fence.

Slide the long arm of the fence into the channel across the front of the shoe and lock it with the wing bolt so that when the T-piece rests against the straight side of the wood the sawing guide notch lies at the right distance from the edge. You have to remember to allow for the width of the kerf and if you are sawing at an angle, for the shift of the actual sawing line away from the line of the guide notch. To avoid mistakes it is always wise to check the angle and depth adjustments and set the rip fence by actual trial on a scrap piece of timber.

Once you are satisfied with the setting of the rip fence the rest is easy. You just keep the fence in contact with the straight side of the wood and advance the saw in the normal way. The rip fence is specially useful when you want to cut a number of battens of the same width from a board or to correct one edge of a plank that is wavy or out of parallel with the other.

You might find that the sliding shoe on the rip fence supplied with the tool is not long enough to prevent the tool from swinging

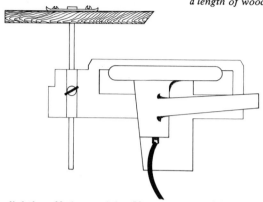

For more accurate rip sawing you can extend the rip fence by screwing on a length of wooden batten.

slightly off the straight. You can extend it and make a big improvement by screwing a length of straight batten on to the inside face of the fence. The Black & Decker rip fence supplied with the saw has two holes in it for this purpose. When you extend the rip fence in this way do not lengthen the back end beyond the centre of the saw blade or the saw may jam if it runs even slightly off line.

You can use the rip fence on either side of the saw but you will notice that the greater width of the shoe lies on the left of the saw blade so the rip fence can be set that much further out on that side than on the right. The fence will adjust to give a width of approximately 6 1/2 in. on the left but only 3 in. on the right. This will not usually worry you because in any case you can always turn the saw around and cut your plank from the other end if you need the extra 3 in. to play with.

However, when you want a guide to help you cut even further than 6 1/2 in. from the edge—e.g. when you want to cut a wide piece off a sheet of plywood or building board—you can lightly nail or clamp a batten to the face of the material and use it to guide the edge of the shoe. This is also a useful dodge when you want to cut across a board at an angle when the rip fence would be useless anyway. And always when cutting large areas of board make sure to arrange to support the whole board on both sides of the sawing line to prevent it from sagging and pinching the blade.

CROSSCUTTING

The combination blade normally supplied with the saw is equally

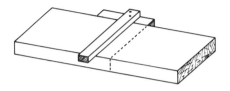

A length of wooden batten lightly nailed to the surface makes a useful guide for cross cutting either straight or at an angle. Nail the batten so that the saw blade follows the required line when the edge of the shoe is kept pressed against it.

good for ripping and crosscutting. However, the rip fence is not a safe guide for cutting straight across a plank because you will generally be cutting too far from the end, or using the saw to get rid of the rough and generally damaged end which would be an unsatisfactory guide anyway.

The answer is to make up a crosscutting guide from a piece of straight batten fastened to a crosspiece to form a T-Square. You can clamp or lightly nail this across the board so that the batten provides a guide for the side of the saw shoe. If you leave the right hand section of the crosspiece long enough, your first cross cut will slice off the surplus and the crosspiece will now provide an accurate guide for future crosscutting. If you place the end of the crosspiece on the sawing line and use the batten to guide the shoe, the saw is bound to cut in the right place.

GROOVING
The circular saw can make an easy job of cutting grooves. First, set the depth of cut to a little less than the depth of the groove. Next make two cuts to mark the outer edges of the groove and follow up with a series of parallel cuts in between, leaving the thinnest possible

wall of wood standing between the cuts. (The rip fence simplifies this part of the job. Don't try to cut away all the wood with the saw or it may tend to slip back into the last cut rather than saw the next slice.) You can clean out the bits you leave standing and smooth off the bottom of the groove with a sharp chisel.

Grooving with a power saw. Left: set saw to depth of groove and make a series of parallel cuts leaving a thin wall of wood between cuts. Centre: Cut away the walls with a wood chisel. Right: Result - a clean, straight groove.

THE SAW BENCH

If your hobby is home carpentry, toy making or any other pastime that calls for accurate sawing, this accessory will more than double the usefulness of your Black & Decker drill and saw attachment by turning them into a bench saw which has many extra advantages. With a bench saw you have a flat work top clear of everything but the actual saw blade and its guard, leaving you with both hands free to manipulate the wood and providing a rip fence for parallel sawing and a mitre guide with a protractor scale for cutting at any angle from $0°$ to $120°$. At the same time the adjustments on the saw attachment still apply: you can alter the depth of cut from 0 in. to 1 1/8 in. and the cutting angle from $0°$ to $45°$ exactly as before. This means that within these limits you have an extremely versatile woodworking tool. The saw bench is supplied as a kit of components with full instructions for assembling to make a sturdy work top supported on four legs, splayed out and cross-stayed to make it rigid. You can either screw the four feet down on to the top of the bench as a permanent fitting (if you can spare the space) or you can fasten them down to a board which you can clamp on to the top of your bench when you plan to have a sawing session. As long as you have a wide enough frame to support the legs, you can cut out the centre section and use the wood for something else. In this case you can clamp the frame to the bench with a timber or channel steel cross-piece bridging the frame and secured by a single wing nut and a bolt passing through a hole drilled in the bench. You can drill other holes in the bench top to allow you a choice of working position for the saw bench depending on the job you have in mind. For instance, one position might be more convenient for ripping up large sheets of ply or hardboard but not for making complicated joints.

The saw attachment, with its rip fence removed or turned over out of the way, is held between four fixed lugs on the underside of the saw bench by a spring-loaded clip which locks the attachment in place automatically when it is pressed home. There is a slot in the top of the bench through which you can insert a screwdriver to release the clip and free the attachment for use as a portable saw.

You may find the top of the saw bench is too small to deal with long or wide panels of timber or board. To get over this you can extend it by making up one or two trestles of the same height as the saw bench and clamping or bolting them to your work bench top to support the overhang; or you can remove the top of the saw bench and let it into the top of your work bench or an old table that you can set up as a permanent saw bench. (See Saw Table, below). However, if you do it this way you will have to dispense with the rip fence and crosscut guide and improvise guides for the timber by nailing battens on to the work top.

This accessory turns a power tool and portable saw attachment into a fixed bench saw without affecting the depth or angle adjustments. It provides an adjustable rip fence and mitring guide.

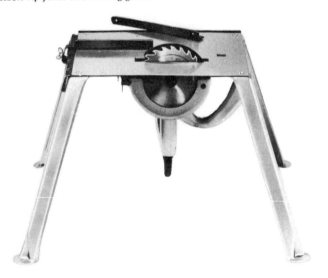

HOW TO USE THE SAW BENCH

With the drill and saw attachment in position on the underside of the bench and the saw blade and guard standing up through the slot you are ready to start sawing. But first check that the saw blade lies on the centre line of the slot and parallel with the sides. Otherwise, edge it one way or the other as necessary with a screwdriver inserted between the side of the shoe and one of the fixed lugs. Check also that the spring loaded clip securing the heel of the attachment shoe is fully engaged and not stuck half way. To be absolutely sure press it firmly into engagement with a screwdriver inserted in the square hole above it.

Finally, never change any of the adjustments without first removing the mains plug from the supply socket and always check that the lower guard is working freely before starting any sawing operations.

For straightforward ripping:

1 Set the rip fence on the left hand side of the bench to the width you want to saw, making allowance for the width of the kerf. (This is always a little more than the thickness of the saw blade and it varies according to the type of blade you are using.)

2 Set the blade angle and depth of cut with the adjustments on the attachment.

3 Press the trigger switch on the drill handle to start the saw and lock it on with the button on the side of the handle.

4 Feed the wood into the saw using your right hand to keep it pressed against the rip fence and your left hand well back from the saw to push it slowly forward.

5 Have about 12 in. of scrap batten handy and when your left hand reaches the front edge of the saw bench, pick up the batten and use it to push the back end of the wood the rest of the way. Make sure your pusher lies to the side of the blade so that it does not run into the teeth when you come to the end of the wood you are ripping.

You may not see the point of the last precaution but even so, make a habit of it. Never try to feed the last of the wood into the saw with your fingers, always do it with a piece of scrap wood. If you do this and the saw runs into a soft spot or the wood splits so that it jumps forward suddenly, your fingers will be safely out of the way.

With some kinds of timber, when you are ripping them on a saw bench, the sawcut closes up and jams against the blade just as it is running out at the other side. As that point of the blade is travelling upwards and towards you it can make the wood you are sawing kick back dangerously.

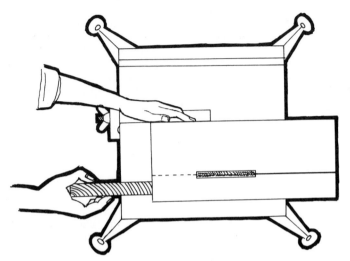

How to use the rip fence for sawing parallel to the edge. Always use a piece of scrap wood to push through the last few inches of wood - never risk doing it with your fingers.

Big circular saws always have a metal 'riving knife' on the exit side of the blade. This keeps the sawcut open and prevents kick back. You are not likely to get an actual kick back with a 5 in. or 6 in. diameter saw, but the sawcut could still squeeze the back of the blade hard enough to slow it down or make it chatter. You can always prevent this from happening by wedging a matchstick or a thin slip of scrap wood into the sawcut behind the saw if you are ripping a long plank.

CROSSCUTTING

The crosscutting guide slides on the rail running along the left hand side of the saw bench. You can set the guide at any angle up to 60° either way using the protractor scale marked on it, but for cross-cutting exactly at right angles to the length of the timber you set the scale to the centre zero position and lock it with the wing nut.

Proceed as follows:

1 Rest the wood to be sawn flat against the guide with the saw mark in line with the blade.

2 Hold the wood firmly in contact with the guide with your left hand and steady it at the other side of the saw mark with your right hand, keeping both hands well away from the saw blade.

3 Press and lock on the trigger switch to start the saw.

4 Advance the wood slowly into the saw with your thumbs pressing against the edge of the wood nearest you.

5 To make sure that the wood parts smoothly, as the saw gets near the end of the cut, press harder with your thumbs as though you were trying to open out the cut. This will stop the sides of the sawcut from gripping the revolving blade and snatching the wood out of your hands. If you are just trimming off a short end, steady the waste with a wooden pusher, not your fingers.

Note: You should never use the rip fence as a guide for normal crosscutting; a lot of dangerous things can happen if you do. The one exception is when the saw is only cutting part way through the timber—e.g. for making a halved joint—when the short end of the timber is not free to fly off or jam at the end of the cut.

CUTTING MITRES

Mitring is crosscutting at an angle instead of straight across the wood. Mostly you will want to cut a mitre at 45°, or half a right angle, so that you can join two mitred ends to make a right angle—·e.g., at the corner of a rectangular frame.

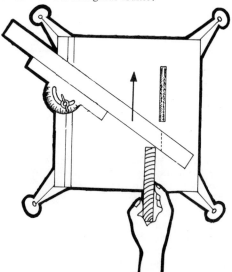

How to use the mitring guide. This guide can also be set at 90° for accurate cross cutting. Here again, use scrap wood for pushing the wood into the saw.

For this operation you set the protractor scale on the mitring guide to 45° and lock it with the wing nut. You can then carry on exactly as you did for crosscutting at right angles. This time, however, you will have to hold the wood very firmly against the guide because the sloping cut will make it tend to bind against one side of the saw and make it run off the sawing line.

It helps if you extend the mitre guide by screwing a suitable length of batten to it using the holes already drilled in the guide for that purpose. Then, if you also clamp the wood to be sawn to the batten, you will be able to cut your mitre without any risk of the blade binding or running off.

Real woodworking enthusiasts can manage the most complex joints by combining the adjustments for cutting depth, width and sawing and mitring angles. But even if you are not a dedicated craftsman, you will find the sawbench and its adjustments a wonderful time-saver on the most ordinary jobs—like making picture frames, boxes, drawers and toys for the youngsters.

CUTTING GROOVES

You can use the saw bench in conjunction with the ripping or crosscutting guide for making accurate grooves and slots by first making saw cuts down each side of the projected groove and then removing slices with a series of intermediate settings, leaving only thin walls between each slice to cut out later with a wood chisel.

THE SAW TABLE

The saw table is the working top of the saw bench without the legs, rip fence or crosscutting and mitring guide. It is designed to be fitted to a hole cut in your bench top to convert it into a saw bench. The method of fixing the drill and saw attachments is the same and there is a slot through which you insert the blade of a screwdriver to free the quick release catch when you want to use the drill and saw attachment away from the bench. You can sink the table flush with the top of your bench when the saw is removed.

Although there is no rip fence or mitring guide, you can always improvise satisfactory substitutes by nailing lengths of batten to the top of your bench to suit the job in hand. The table does not interfere with the normal depth and sawing angle adjustments on the attachment.

Both the saw bench and the saw table are designed to hold an adaptor which lets you mount the Black & Decker jigsaw—or a drill with jigsaw attachment—underneath. (See the section on jigsaws.)

BLACK & DECKER INTEGRAL SAW

There are two Black & Decker home user portable power saw units: one is a purpose-designed, integral power saw, taking a 6 in. saw blade; the other is, strictly speaking, not an integral tool but an assembly of the Black & Decker portable saw attachment on the single speed power drill body, and takes a 5 in. saw blade. The second saw costs less than the true integral saw. The arrangement offers you a reliable saw at an extremely low price if you do not have enough use for a circular saw to justify the greater cost of the larger integral saw. While the assembly does not have the same performance as the complete unit it has advantages of its own, apart from its low cost, that could still make it your first choice—e.g. you can add a further attachment so that you can use it as a bench saw and still add any of the other attachments or accessories that screw in place of the chuck—including the disc and finishing sanders, jigsaw attachment and polishing heads.

The Black & Decker integral circular saw. This type of power tool is the one to buy when you have to saw timber too heavy or awkward to handle on a bench saw. It has an adjustable rip fence, angle and depth adjustments and can be used for rip sawing and cross cutting.

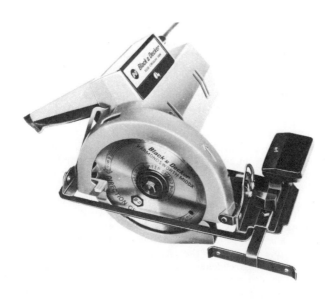

The integral circular saw is designed as a powerful but completely portable piece of equipment, easy to handle and adjust for depth and angle of cut. You would buy this model if you had a lot of serious sawing to do such as ripping up long planks or doing a lot of crosscutting of timber into short sections, especially where you could not bring the work into the workshop and do the job on a bench saw. It is the perfect tool for the small builder or the do-it-yourself enthusiast who wants to build his own garage or workshop or put an extension on the side of his house.

The saw is based on a powerful, 350 watt motor and gearbox housed in an alloy case with a pistol grip handle incorporating an on-off trigger switch. The 6 in. circular saw blade is mounted on the right-hand side of the gearbox and protected by an upper guard which is one with the gearbox cover and a spring loaded lower guard which normally covers the lower segment of the blade but retracts automatically when the saw is advanced into the work. With this arrangement the teeth of the revolving blade are only exposed at the point where the wood is being sawn so there is no risk of getting your fingers caught accidentally. You have to swing the lower guard out of the way to fit or remove the blade but you should never do this, or make any adjustments whatsoever, while the saw is plugged into the mains. This is one of the things that you are always tempted to do when you are in a hurry but that is the very time when you ought to be more careful than usual, not less.

The saw unit rests on a flat steel shoe in which there is a long slot through which the blade and its lower **guard** project. At its front end the shoe is pivoted to the case so that the saw can be raised or lowered by tilting it up or down. This tilt increases or decreases the projection of the blade below the shoe and so controls the depth of cut. You can lock the saw at any desired depth of cut with a wing nut and bolt sliding in a quadrant at the back of the shoe.

The shoe is also pivoted at each end so that the saw can be tilted sideways to cut at an angle. The angle of the saw is indicated on a protractor scale at the front end of the shoe and a wing nut locks it in any position from a 5° tilt to the left to a 45° tilt to the right. The scale is marked in 5° steps, 0° being the setting at which the saw blade is at right angles to the surface of the work.

The front of the shoe also has a cross-ways channel to take a rip fence. This is a T-shaped piece of metal which forms an adjustable guide for sawing parallel to the straight edge of a board or plank. The long arm of the T slides into the channel and can be locked by a wing bolt. The crosspiece is formed as a flat shoe with the ends curved out so that it slides easily along the edge of the wood. The rip fence may be fitted into the slot from either side so that you can use it for sawing to right or left of the edge of the wod.

A flat headed knob is screwed to the front end of the shoe to provide a hand hold in addition to the pistol grip on the motor casing.

ASSEMBLING THE SAW

The saw is supplied complete except for the 3-pin plug which you will need to connect the cable to the mains (p 164). The only loose item, apart from the rip fence, is the saw blade which you will have to fit before you can use the saw.

If you find it difficult to fit the saw blade over the washer according to the instructions in the leaflet, here is an easier way: First fit the washer into the centre of the saw blade and make it stick there with a dab of thick grease or a couple of strips of Sellotape, then slide the blade into position over the hole and carry on as above.

HOW TO USE THE CIRCULAR SAW

The depth of cut, angle and rip fence adjustments on the integral saw follow the pattern already described for the circular saw attachment and the method of operation is the same. However, one thing you can do with the integral saw that you cannot do with the attachment is pocket cutting. You can do this with the integral saw because the large hand grip on the front of the shoe gives you a firmer grip of the unit and because the lower guard has a positive, spring-loaded return.

You may not want to do pocket cutting often, but when you do, it is such a great time saver that it is described in detail below.

POCKET CUTTING

You use the pocket cutting technique when you want to start your cut in the face of a board—e.g. when you want to open up tongue and grooved flooring or cut a rectangular hole in a wood panel. This operation can be such a time saver that it is well worth mastering.

As usual you should look out a piece of scrap timber to practise on—say a piece 1/2 in. to 1 in. thick, and for your first attempts make sure that everything is as it should be before you press the trigger:

1 Set up the trial wood so that it is firmly fixed and with space below it to allow the saw blade to run out, e.g. nail a piece of board to form a bridge between two battens fixed to the bench, or clamp it to the top of the bench with enough overhang to work on.

(Pocket cutting with a jigsaw is discussed on p 76.)

2 With the lead unplugged from the mains set the depth of the saw to a little more than the thickness of your piece of wood. (This is most important when you are sawing into floorboards which may be covering wiring or pipes.)

3 Make sure that the mains lead will start and stay well out of the way of the tool.

4 Turn the lower guard back to its full open position using the projecting stop on the side of the guard so that your fingers are always well away from the teeth.

5 Rest the back edge of the shoe plate on the trial wood and release the lower guard.

6 Tilt the tool forward until the saw blade is just clear of the surface of the wood. (You should really practise getting to this point for a while before you plug in the mains lead.)

7 Press the trigger switch and carefully lower the saw while maintaining pressure on the back edge of the shoe.

8 Hold the tool firmly as the blade cuts its way through the board and do not slide it forward until the shoe is flat on the surface.

9 Release the trigger switch and allow the saw to come to rest before you lift it out of the cut.

After you have made some experimental cuts both with and across the grain, mark a sawing line on the wood and practise until you can cut along it. When cutting out a panel, if you do not want saw cuts to show at the corners you will have to stop the saw blade when it reaches the corner and use a padsaw to cut away the remaining wood left by the curvature of the circular blade.

BLADES FOR YOUR CIRCULAR SAW

Strictly speaking, you need one type of saw blade for ripping timber (sawing it along the grain) and another type for crosscutting. The ripsaw blade has coarse chisel-edge teeth which take a big bite and let you saw along the grain at really high speed. This type of tooth does not leave a smooth finish, but the edge of the wood is usually planed smooth afterwards so a rough sawcut is not a disadvantage.

The crosscut blade has a tougher job to do since it has to sever all the thin hard ridges of the grain as it cuts its way across. A ripsaw blade with its big bite would make heavy work of crosscutting but more important, it would tear the grain instead of making a clean cut. It would leave the end of the timber rough, and you cannot plane end grain smooth without a lot of experience and trouble. That is why, for crosscutting where you want to leave the surface with a smooth finish, you use a special crosscut saw blade with teeth that are finer and also ground to cut on the side as well as the tip of the tooth.

Black & Decker power saws and attachments are normally supplied with a combination of rip and crosscut type of blade. This has teeth of an intermediate form which will rip timber along the grain as fast as you are ever likely to want to saw but at the same time will leave a reasonably smooth finish when used for cutting across the grain. This arrangement saves you the inconvenience of having to change over blades when you want to do ripping and crosscutting with the same tool.

However, if you want to leave an extra good finish and do really accurate crosscutting and mitring, you can buy a blade designed specifically for that job, but you will have to accept a slower rate of sawing. In any event you should never use this type of blade for cutting with the grain, especially with resinous timbers because the higher friction can seriously overload and perhaps damage the motor as well as slowing down the rate of sawing.

In addition to the ripping and crosscut blades described above, there are many other types of blade to fit your circular saw or attachment for doing specialised jobs. These blades include the following:

Tungsten carbide tipped blades. These are available for most sawing applications and have a very much longer life than the ordinary steel blades they replace. Naturally they cost more, but if you do a lot of sawing—particularly of hard or abrasive timbers, laminates, Conti-board and similar manufactured boards—they are worth the extra.

Planer blade. This type is hollow ground to give a fine smooth finish on all wood laminated plastics and man-made boards, and cuts out intermediate planing operations.

Flooring blade. For sawing wood which may have occasional nails in it and for harder, resinous bondings like plywood and blockboard.

Metal cutting blade. Cuts aluminium, copper, lead and other soft metals.

Abrasive disc. (Silicon Carbide). A flexible and shatter resistant disc for cutting asbestos, marble, slate, ceramics etc.

Abrasive disc. (Aluminium Oxide). Similar to above, for cutting thin gauge ferrous metals—e.g. drain pipes, gutters, steel cables, etc.

Do not expect your Black & Decker dealer to have all the blades in stock but he will usually be able to get the one you want in a day or two.

KEEPING BLADES SHARP

Feel the teeth of a new saw blade and notice how razor sharp they are and how shining and bright the whole blade looks. This is how a blade should always be or it isn't worth using, first because a dull or rusty blade puts an extra load on the motor and may overheat and damage it, and next because its speed of cutting falls off and it doesn't give as clean a cut. If you have any trouble at all in using a circular saw the odds are that either the teeth have lost their keen edge or the blade is dull and rusted or gummed up with a dirty film of old oil. Blunt teeth and a sticky blade slow down the motor and cause overheating; you have to push the saw harder to make it cut and this can make it run off the line. Unless the blade is in first-class shape, the whole performance of the saw deteriorates.

Sharpening a circular saw blade is a job for an expert, but there is no need for you to attempt it yourself, just take the old blade back to your Black & Decker dealer who will get it re-sharpened like new for less than half the price of a new blade. If you do this, your saw will give you longer trouble-free service and you will be able to do a cleaner, quicker job with it.

You can work your circular saw hard and still preserve the sharp edge on the teeth for a very long time by taking a little trouble. First see that any wood you cut is clean and dry. If you are using up old timber, brush any dirt or grit off the surface first and take a good look around it for nails or screws or bits of metal fastenings that may have been broken off and left behind. When you are using your saw, keep the blade moving steadily into the wood; do not let it rest in the cut while still running as this tends to heat the blade and blunt the teeth. Always set the depth of cut so that the teeth just run out of the timber—if the blade projects more than this it puts an unnecessary load on the motor because the teeth act less efficiently and the friction between the blade and the sides of the saw cut is greater. Do not try to change the direction of the blade once it starts sawing or you will jam the blade and be in trouble. Finally, before you put the saw away, wipe the blade clean and give it a smear of thin oil to keep it bright. Remember that it is wise to do everything possible to prevent the saw blade from putting an extra load on the drill motor which is doing a big job already.

THE JIGSAW ATTACHMENT AND INTEGRAL
   POWER JIGSAW

A jigsaw lets you cut around curves whereas a circular saw can only cut in a straight line. This is because the jigsaw blade is a narrow toothed strip of metal 3/8 in. or so wide. It moves up and down several thousand times a minute so it cuts quickly and it can be guided around quite tight curves; in fact you can easily cut out a circle smaller than 1 in. diameter. At the same time you can use a jigsaw for cutting straight lines although it takes much longer than with a circular saw of the same power.

Jigsaw blades are made in various tooth pitches from fine to coarse, and by choosing the correct one you can saw soft or hard woods, laminates, plastics and sheet metal. There is even a plain knife blade that you can use for cutting leather, fabric and plastic or rubber foam.

As with the portable circular saws, you can either use your power drill to drive a jigsaw attachment, or you can buy a jigsaw designed as an integral tool, complete with its own motor, gearbox and jigsaw mechanism. The attachment is the obvious choice if you want to keep the cost down and do not mind changing attachments to suit the job.

The Black & Decker jigsaw attachment and the integral jigsaw described below are typical of this class of power tool and whatever your make of electric drill it is almost certain that there is a jigsaw attachment available for it. The Black & Decker attachment, being designed to clamp on to the body of the power tool is obviously preferable to the type where the driving spindle of the attachment is simply gripped in the chuck of the power tool.

THE BLACK & DECKER JIGSAW ATTACHMENT

The jigsaw attachment is designed to convert any Black & Decker drill listed in the equipment pages at the back of the book into a jigsaw which will give the same performance as the integral jigsaw. If you are only likely to use a jigsaw occasionally and you do not mind the small amount of trouble involved in the changeover, then the jigsaw attachment is a better investment. In operation the jigsaw attachment is identical with the integral jigsaw except that it gets its power from the drill motor instead of from its own built-in motor. And it costs less because you do not have to pay for a second motor.

The Black & Decker jigsaw attachment turns any Black & Decker home user power tool into a jigsaw for making straight or curved cuts in wood, plastics, laminates and metal.

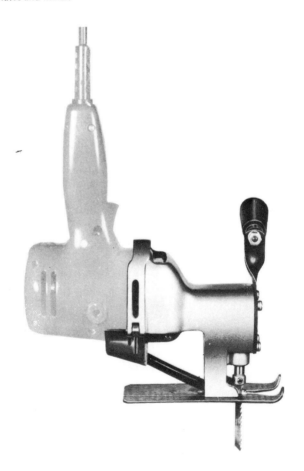

HOW TO FIT THE JIGSAW ATTACHMENT

Before you can fit the jigsaw attachment, you have to remove the drill chuck. To do this, disconnect the drill from the power socket and make sure that the trigger switch is released. Point the drill away from you, fit the chuck key in the drill and give it a smart downward tap with a block of wood or a light hammer. This will free the chuck on its thread and you can then unscrew it. You then screw the drive adaptor into the drill spindle in place of the chuck. (For fuller details on this operation see p 23.) You are now ready to fit the jigsaw attachment. Here is how to do it:

1 Unscrew the nut from the hook bolt on the adaptor until you can turn the hook round to the slot in the top half of the adaptor.

2 Open the hinged clamp.

3 Insert the nose of the drill with the handle upper-most so that the drive adaptor fits into the slot in the drive coupling and the square lugs on the attachment case fit into the slots in the front of the drill case. (Some drills have more than one ring of slots but you always use the foremost ring which is the one nearest to the chuck.)

4 Make sure all the square lugs are lodged in the slot and close the clamp.

5 Turn the hook bolt so that the hook lies in the groove in the case and tighten the wing nut.

6 Fasten the handle to the bracket on the front of the attachment with the nut and washer supplied. Normally you fit the handle to the right of the tool but if you are left handed it will fit just as easily. the other way round.

GETTING THE SAW READY

With the jigsaw attachment you use an Allen key for tightening the setscrews that hold the saw blade in the saw chuck. This key is a length of hexagonal section steel which fits into the hexagonal recess in the head of the setscrew. It is bent at right angles so that you can fit one arm into the setscrew and use the other to turn it for tightening or slackening the screw. You get extra leverage when you insert the short arm in the setscrew and use the long arm for tightening but do not overdo it or you may damage the blade or the screw.

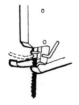

The blade fits in the holder with the teeth pointing upwards. It is held in place by 2 setscrews tightened with an Allen key as shown.

You will have to fit the blade yourself and this is how you do it:

1 Insert the blade in the saw chuck at the front end of the tool with the teeth facing forward.

2 If necessary slack off the two setscrews with the Allen key so that the plain end of the saw can be pushed right home.

3 Turn both setscrews with the Allen key—front screw first—until you have taken up all the slack in the thread and the screw is up against the blade.

4 Tighten the front setscrew firmly and then the side setscrew.

You will notice that the teeth of the saw blade point towards the tool. This is so that the thrust of the saw acts against the shoe and is independent of any pressure you may exert. In this way the action of the saw is balanced—there is no push or pull on your hand; all you have to do is to guide the saw where you want it to go.

HOW TO USE THE JIGSAW ATTACHMENT

While you can operate the integral jigsaw with one hand, you have to use two to control the jigsaw attachment mounted on the power drill. One hand, usually the right, holds the drill handle (now pointing upwards) and operates the on-off trigger switch. The other hand grasps the handle on the attachment. And as both hands are occupied it is most important to clamp the wood you are cutting firmly to the top of the bench.

If your drill is a 2-speed or variable speed model, set it to its highest speed when sawing wood as a lower saw blade speed will tend to tear the wood instead of cutting it cleanly. However, when you are cutting sheet metal your blade will have an easier time and stay sharp longer if you use low speed.

After a long spell of hard sawing check the wing nut for tightness.

When you remove the attachment and want to replace the drill chuck, grip the flat key of the drive adaptor in the jaws of an adjustable spanner and give the handle a light tap to loosen the screw just as you did the drill chuck key to loosen the chuck. Make sure that the fibre washer is still in position on the drive adaptor for the next time you want to use it.

With an integral jigsaw you can cut along intricate curves down to a radius of 1/4 in. or less. (See p. 79).

LUBRICATION

After every 15 min. or so of use, lubricate the drive and blade spindles with a drop or two of light machine oil.

HOW TO USE THE JIGSAW WITH WOOD

As usual, it is wise to practise on a piece of scrap board before attempting any serious sawing. Clamp an odd piece of board on top of the bench so that the part you are going to saw hangs over the edge. Now rest the front end of the shoe on the edge of the wood with the teeth of the saw just clear. Hold the shoe down firmly and press the trigger switch in the handle to start the saw.

The high speed vibration will probably startle you at first but you will soon get used to it. Now, while still keeping the shoe firmly in contact with the wood, push the saw forward. The blade will cut easily into the wood and as it does so the vibration of the tool will become much less noticeabe.

When you have cut an inch in a straight line, slowly turn the saw first one way and then the other as you move it forward until you get the feel of it. Now switch off the saw, withdraw it from the cut and draw a curve on the wood with a pencil. Now try to follow the line accurately with the saw. Practise sawing so that the cut just skims the line you have drawn, keeping the saw always on the waste wood side of the line. You will soon be able to cut around the most intricate curves with ease. If you always saw along the side of the line it will be there for reference when you finally smooth off the edge. You should make allowance for the thickness of the line when you mark it on the wood so that the size will be right if you do not cut away the line.

When you are practising—and in fact at any other time—remember that the blade of the saw needs a clear run underneath the material you are sawing as well as on top. You do not want to carve pieces out of your bench top or ruin the saw blade by trying to cut through the jaws of your vice so you need some form of holding device which you can release easily when you want to move the wood around as the saw progresses. This is where you will find a bench holdfast or the Black & Decker quick release clamp useful (p 108.) An alternative is to fix the jigsaw on the bench (see Jigsaw Adaptor Plate, p 81) and move the wood into the saw.

The jigsaw is chiefly intended for freehand sawing along curves but you can cut straight lines accurately if you clamp a steel straight-edge or a straight strip of batten to the surface to act as a guide to the side of the shoe. The Black & Decker jigsaw attachment instruction leaflet describes a suitable guide that is well worth making up if you are going to do a lot of straight sawing. It is made from a straight batten with a cross piece fastened on the end and looking like a draughtsman's T-square. To make a straight cut across a plank or board you first use the batten to draw the saw line, setting it square with the cross piece. Next you move the batten to the left so that when you hold the left hand side of the shoe against it, the saw blade is opposite the line you have just drawn. Now make your saw cut, keeping the side of the shoe pressed against the batten.

If you leave enough spare on the cross piece and run the saw right off the end, it will cut it at just the right length to act as a sawing guide in future. Set the end of the cross piece against your sawing line and the batten automatically lies in the correct position to guide the saw blade along the line, with the right amount of displacement to allow for the width of the shoe.

Once you have set the batten square with the edge of the wood you can either clamp the batten on to the wood you are cutting or nail it down lightly. If you want to make a real job of your sawing guide you can make the cross piece adjustable so that you can set it for sawing at, say, $30°$, $45°$, $60°$ and $90°$.

POCKET CUTTING

When you cut a complete shape out of the centre of a piece of wood leaving the surrounding wood intact, this is known as pocket cutting. The usual way of tackling this operation is to drill a hole on the waste side of the centre piece big enough to let you insert the saw blade and start your cut. However, with the Black & Decker jigsaw there is no need to drill a starting hole. You can actually saw your way in. (This is specially useful when you are using a power drill with the jigsaw attachment. It is a nuisance to have to remove the attachment and replace the chuck before you can start another hole.)

Here is the way to do it and, once again, practise on a piece of scrap wood:

1 Rest the tips of the shoe plate on the surface of the wood with the tool tilted up so that the end of the saw is well clear of the wood. (Remember to allow an extra 5/8 in. clearance if the saw has stopped at the top of its stroke.)

2 Grasp the tool firmly with one hand gripping the handle and the other holding the back of the tool to steady it.

3 Press the trigger switch and with the saw running, slowly reduce the tilt on the tool to bring the moving blade down on to the surface, keeping the tips of the shoe firmly in place.

4 As the saw blade begins to enter the wood, let the tips of the shoe slide back until the flat part of the shoe plate is resting on the surface and the saw is running freely right through the wood. (When in this position the blade will have cut a slit about 3/4 in. in the top, widening to 1 1/4 in. on the underside, so you cannot use this method if you want to keep the saw cut inside a 1 in. circle.)

5 Carry on sawing in the usual way, taking care to keep the saw cut on the waste side of the line. (This will depend on whether the cut out piece or the surrounding wood is the important item.) After a few attempts you will be able to pierce the wood right against the sawing line.

There is no need to start cutting at the edge of the wood. You can cut straight into the surface this way.

How to cut out a rectangular opening with the jigsaw, starting with a pocket cut as shown on left.

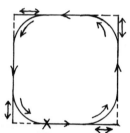

If the pocket you are cutting has a continuous outline with no sharp corners, you can simply carry on sawing until you get back to where you started and the cut out piece will drop away. However, if you are cutting out an angular shape like a triangle or square it is not quite as simple because the width of the blade stops you from turning it at a sharp angle. So here is what you do:

1 Saw to the line right in to the first corner.

2 Back the saw about 1/2 in. away from the corner, taking care to keep it running in the saw cut.

3 Start sawing again in a curve so that you by-pass the corner and join the line again on the other side.

4 Saw right into the next corner, then back the saw away and repeat the above procedure until you get back to the start.

5 The cut-out part will come away leaving pieces of waste timber still attached at each corner.

6 Reverse the direction of the saw and cut away the waste pieces by sawing back along the line right into each corner. (Pocket cutting with a circular saw is discussed on p 67).

LAMINATES

When you are cutting a large sheet of thin ply wood or hardboard secure it firmly to prevent it from fluttering with the motion of the saw and keep it level; if you let it sag the sides of the saw cut may pinch the blade and make sawing difficult. Always stop the tool before you lift the saw blade out of the cut.

When you saw any of the manufactured boards with a laminated finish of plastics or veneer, do not forget that the jigsaw cuts on the upstroke and will tend to splinter away the finish if it is on top. This material should be sawn with the finish underneath, using a fine blade and advancing the saw slowly.

If the board is veneered on both sides it is better to mark the cutting lines in pencil and cut through the veneer with a sharp knife. This avoids splintering the veneer; or you can prevent splintering by sticking transparent 'Sellotape' over the cutting lines on each side.

You may find on making a test cut on an unwanted corner (which you should do anyway) that you will get a cleaner cut if you clamp a piece of scrap board under the laminate face and saw through the whole sandwich at once. If the board is supplied with a protective layer of self-adhesive paper or plastic sheeting over the laminate, leave this in position until you have finished sawing.

Thin sheet metal or plastics should be clamped between scrap wood before jigsawing.

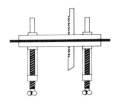

Cut veneered wood with the veneer underneath to prevent splintering.

METAL

With the correct Black & Decker saw blades you can cut the softer metals—aluminium, brass and copper—in sheet form up to about 1/16 in. thick as readily as wood. If the sheet is very thin it may flutter and tear leaving a ragged cut with a wavy edge. The answer is to clamp it to a flat piece of waste wood and saw the two together. However, metal as thin as this can usually be cut with tin snips.

If you try to cut sheet metal more than about 1/16 in. thick, you run the risk of overloading the motor and shortening the life of the blade. And whatever kind of sheet metal you cut, a smear of ordinary lubricating oil along the saw line will help to lighten the load on the motor and lengthen the life of the blade.

THE BLACK & DECKER INTEGRAL POWER JIGSAW

The Black & Decker integral power jigsaw is for the man who has a lot of use for this type of tool and doesn't want the trouble of fitting an attachment to his power tool.

This is a self-contained power tool designed solely for jigsawing. It does the same job as the jigsaw attachment and, in fact, the business end is more or less the same. However, the power jigsaw is more compact and easier to manipulate than the power drill and attachment. If you are likely to want to do much sawing around curves in wood, plastics or sheet metal, it will pay you to choose the integral tool. Or if you dislike changing attachments and belong to the 'one-job-one-tool' school, then the modest extra cost of the integral jigsaw will be well worth paying.

A moulded case houses the motor and the mechanism that converts the rotary movement of the armature to the up and down movement of the saw. There is a handle with an on-off trigger switch and lock-on button over the motor housing and a flat steel shoe below to allow the jigsaw to slide over the surface of the material being cut.

The saw blade is clamped in a holder by two setscrews, one in front and one on the left hand side. These are tightened with an Allen key in the same way as the setscrews on the jigsaw attachment.

When you switch the motor on the blade moves up and down in the throat of a V-shaped opening in the leading end of the shoe. This arrangement lets you watch the cutting edge of the saw blade as you slide it forward to follow a guide line. Part of the draught from the motor cooling fan blows on to the front of the saw blade to clear away the sawdust so that you can always see what you are doing.

HOW TO USE THE JIGSAW

The integral power jigsaw is used in exactly the same way as the jigsaw attachment. It can be used for pocket cutting and for straight sawing either freehand along a ruled line or guided by a batten nailed or clamped to the top of the work.

THE JIGSAW BLADES

There are 6 interchangeable blades made for the jigsaw and jigsaw attachment: a knife blade for cutting rubber, plastic foam, fabric and so on, coarse and fine blades both for metal and for wood, and a general purpose blade for all-round sawing of soft and hard woods, plastics, manufactured boards, light alloys and so on. This is the one to buy if you do not do a lot of jigsawing and want one blade to do everything. Otherwise you should buy the blade recommended for the material you want to saw. In general, the harder the metal or wood, the finer the sawblade you should use, although for aluminium, copper and light alloys, which tend to clog the teeth instead of blowing clear, it is usually better to use the coarsest of the metal cutting blades.

LUBRICATION

There are oil wick holes on each side at the front of the casing and one at the back. You should run 4 to 6 drops of light machine oil into each of the front holes and a drop or two into the rear hole at the end of every working session or in any case once every 15−30 working minutes.

CARBON BRUSHES

See information under this heading in Power Tool Electrics

MAINTENANCE

Apart from regular lubrication and keeping a check on the condition of the carbon brushes the power jigsaw requires no maintenance. However, as with all power tools used for woodwork you should inspect the ventilation slits in the motor housing to see that they are not choked with wood dust. Up to a point you can keep the passages clear with a narrow, long-bristled paint brush, but every 12 months or so, if you are using the tool regularly, you should return it to your Black & Decker Service Centre to be stripped down and thoroughly cleaned.

JIGSAW ADAPTOR PLATE

Both the saw bench and saw table (described in the section on Black & Decker circular saws) are designed to take an adaptor so you can mount the jigsaw, or a drill fitted with the jigsaw attachment, underneath so that the saw blade projects through an opening in the work top. With this arrangement you can cut complicated shapes by moving the work into the saw blade as you would when using a fretsaw or bandsaw.

When you use the jigsaw in this way you must feed the work into the saw carefully, giving it plenty of time to clear itself and thus prevent it from jamming and lifting the work off the table. For the same reason you should saw very slowly around tight turns. The noisy clattering that goes on when the saw carries the work with it is not likely to cause any damage but it interferes with your control of the work and sounds more serious than it really is.

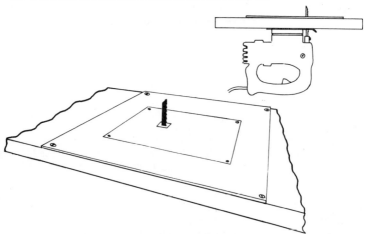

The jigsaw adaptor plate turns the integral jigsaw into a bench mounted tool which leaves both your hands free for manipulating the material you are sawing.

SANDERS AND SANDING

One of the most useful things about power tools is the way they take the sweat out of working with sandpaper and other kinds of abrasive sheet. It is surprising how many jobs around the house, workshop and garage involve some sort of sanding operation, from smoothing woodwork after sawing or shaping, getting it ready for painting, rubbing down primer or undercoat, shaping resin filler or glass fibre, right down to easing sticking doors, windows or drawers. Sanding in some shape or form has always been a tough and tiring job when you have to do it by hand but nowadays power tools have made it quick and effortless. Furthermore, today powered sanding is not just a way of smoothing and finishing, it is a flexible and versatile way of shaping too. Ordinary sandpaper was all right in the old days when you used it by hand but it does not stand up to the speeds and fast cutting rates that you get with power tools, so the industry has come up with specially developed abrasive sheet materials which cut faster, last longer and do not clog like ordinary sandpaper.

There are all sorts of ways of applying the abrasive sheet to the job and all sorts of power tools for doing it. However, the most popular sanding tools for the home user are: (a) the two types of abrasive disc sander, flexible and rigid, that you spin round in place of the chuck of your power drill and (b) the finishing sander, also known as an orbital sander because the shoe holding the abrasive sheet moves around in tiny circles or 'orbits'.

The disc sanders are designed primarily for shaping and rounding off woodwork (although they have many other uses) and the finishing sanders for getting a satin smooth finish on surfaces that you are going to paint.

The thing to remember is that you use a rotary sander to remove stock, for jobs that you would otherwise do with a rasp, spokeshave or similar tool. You use a finishing sander principally to get rid of surface roughness in readiness for painting or varnishing, the sort of job that you would otherwise do with a sheet of sandpaper wrapped around a block of wood.

If you try to remove a lot of material with a finishing sander you just clog the abrasive surface because the dust cannot get away as it can from a disc sander. One exception to this rule is the use of a finishing sander for flatting down rough plaster or patches of Poly-filla. In this case, however, you use a coarse abrasive sheet with a very open coating which allows plenty of room for the powdered plaster to collect without impairing the cutting action.

You can do disc sanding with any electric power drill by simply fitting the spindle of the sanding disc in the chuck in place of a drill. When you come to finishing sanders you can buy a finishing sander attachment for a power drill or an integral power tool designed specifically for the job. In the following pages you can read all about these different types of sander, the sort of jobs they are suitable for, and how to use them.

One type of disc sanding pad screws into the power tool in place of the chuck to make a compact sanding tool.

An alternative type has a short spindle which can be held in the drill chuck. This adds to the overall length of the tool and makes it more awkward to handle.

FLEXIBLE DISC SANDERS

A flexible disc sander is just a circle of abrasive material backed by a moulded rubber pad which you spin round with a power drill. It sounds, and is, a very simple sort of tool but next to the drill itself it is probably bought by more home handymen than any other power tool accessory. It is versatile, easy to use and you can set yourself up with the whole outfit for the price of a couple of packets of cigarettes. It is also completely portable; you can use it anywhere.

This Black & Decker flexible disc sander has a threaded shank to screw in place of the chuck on any Black and Decker home user power tool.

The speed of the sanding disc, usually somewhere between 1,500 and 2,500 r.p.m. gives it tremendous cutting power while the flexibility of the backing enables it to wrap around corners and flex into hollows if you want it to. So if you are sanding a curved object like the arm of a chair or rubbing down plastic filler repair in a dented motor car wing, you can apply it so that it shapes itself to the curves and does not leave flat places on the rounded surface. On the other hand you can use it equally well for smoothing flat surfaces. So you can see that a flexible sander can easily double the usefulness of your power drill.

THE BLACK & DECKER FLEXIBLE DISC SANDER

There are two moulded rubber flexible backing discs made to fit the whole range of Black & Decker power drills. One has a centre spindle that fits in the drill chuck like an ordinary drill bit. The other has a threaded spigot that screws into the drill spindle in place of the chuck. The discs themselves are identical but you will probably find it easier to use the one that screws in place of the chuck because being closer to the body of the drill, it is easier to control. On the other hand, if you just want to do a quick bit of sanding and then get back to drilling, it is less trouble to use the spindle type and leave the chuck in position.

In both types the rubber backing disc has a shallow recess in the front face to take a conical metal washer held in place by a countersunk screw. This centre fitting is used to receive the abrasive disc.

The abrasive discs are just a bit bigger across than the rubber backing so that you can use them right up to the edge. The centre of the disc has a hole to take the fixing screw and the edge of the hole is slit so that it can fit into the depressed centre of the rubber moulding without tearing or wrinkling.

This is how to fit the sander:

1 Fit the rubber backing disc in the drill. According to the type of disc, either remove the chuck (p 23) and screw in the threaded spigot, or grip the plain spindle in the jaws of the chuck like a drill.

2 Remove the screw and washer from the centre of the backing disc with a screwdriver.

3 Hold the abrasive disc, rough side out, flat on the face of the backing disc, and secure it with the screw and washer.

4 The sander is now ready for use.

HOW TO USE THE SANDER

First make sure that the thing you want to sand is held securely. If it is not already part of a solid structure—e.g. a door jamb, a table top or a motor car body—then fix it to a firm support. For a start it would be wise to practise on a piece of scrap wood. You can grip it in a vice, clamp it down on to the top of a bench or nail it down temporarily. (When you do this take care to position the nails so that the holes will not show on the finished article.)

Next hold the drill firmly in both hands, one on the pistol grip and the other on the side handle, and switch on. Now bring the sanding disc into contact with the surface to be sanded, tilting it so that it only bears on one side while the other runs clear of the surface. But do not tilt it at such a steep angle that the edge of the disc cuts into the surface. If you are practising on scrap wood you can find out by trial how easy it is to do this.

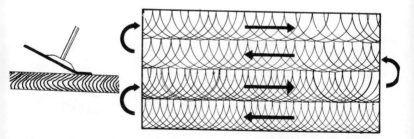

When sanding a flat area tilt the power tool so that only half the disc is in contact with the surface. Then work over the surface with long, zig-zag sweeps.

The important thing in power sanding is to keep the sander moving. Work with a continuous to and fro action. Never let the sander stay in one place or it will cut a hollow that will take a lot of extra work to level up. For your first trials stick to wide flat surfaces and just press lightly on the tool. The sander shifts a lot of material and absorbs a lot of power so it is very easy to overload the motor by putting too much pressure on the disc.

Another reason for only pressing lightly and keeping the sander moving is that in this way you make it easier to get rid of the dust. If you press the disc hard on one spot, the dust gets trapped and soon clogs the spaces between the grains of abrasive. When that happens the disc stops cutting and if you try to counteract the clogging by pressing any harder the resulting friction will eventually char the surface.

Because the rubber backing disc is flexible, it tends to wrap itself around sharp edges that get in its way and in a very short time there is no edge left. So if you want to preserve the edge of the surface— e.g. the top of a table or the face of a plank—you have to apply the disc to the surface so that the part in contact runs away from the edge all the time and never towards it.

If you want to sand away an edge or a sharp corner, then come at it from behind. Start on the flat and then work towards and over the edge so that the disc does not run straight into the sharp angle. Unless you do it this way you run the risk of tearing the abrasive disc. A sanding disc will last for a considerable time so long as you do not use it to make a direct attack on sharp edges and corners.

The flexible disc sander has many other uses apart from shaping and smoothing woodwork. You can use the normal abrasive disc for smoothing masonry, de-rusting metal surfaces, cleaning up exterior brick and stone facings and even for shaping ceramic tiles to fit around pipework and sanitary fittings in the bathroom and kitchen.

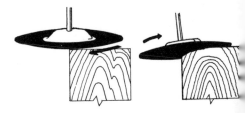

To prevent the sander from rounding a sharp edge hold the tool so that the operative half of the disc runs off -not into-the edge.

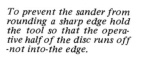

For the tougher materials you can buy special abrasive discs which will cut practically anything, including glass, and which you can also use for sharpening tools although this job can be done better with the rigid disc sander attachment described later.

While the sander is mostly used for free hand work, holding it in your hands, for many jobs it is more effective if you fix it on a firm support leaving both hands free to hold the work. There are two Black & Decker stands that let you do this, the horizontal stand holds the drill horizontally on the bench and the vertical drill stand holds it in a carriage sliding on a vertical pillar clamped or screwed down to the bench. The horizontal stand is the more useful for bench mounted sanding operations, the vertical stand is designed principally for converting your portable drill into a bench drill.

You can mount the horizontal drill stand on your bench so that the sanding disc faces towards you in the most convenient position for sanding objects small enough to hold in your hands, from a chair leg to a piece of dolls' house furniture. This way you can use your sander for creative woodwork as it leaves you free to shape flowing curves and other interesting shapes.

The standard procedure in all sanding operations is to use a coarse abrasive for rough shaping and gradually move on to finer and finer grades, each removing the scratches left by the one before, until you arrive at the quality of finish you require. Obviously, you will go on to create a smoother finish where the final job will be natural waxed or oiled wood than if you are just preparing the surface for painting.

Remember that you can fit another flexible back in your drill quicker than you can change the abrasive disc—and with less risk of damage to the disc. So it pays to buy *two* flexible backs, one for the coarser and the other for the finer abrasive disc.

RIGID DISC SANDERS

One of the nice things about a flexible back disc sander is the way it bends around curved surfaces like the arms and legs on furniture or the bodywork of a car. But for some sorts of work flexibility is a disadvantage. If you want to make a surface flat and with square corners, or you want to put a flat bevel on a square corner, the flexible backed disc will not help you. However, there is another type that will and this is the rigid disc sander. In the Black & Decker Accessories list this appears as the Metal Sanding and Sharpening Plate.

THE BLACK & DECKER METAL SANDING AND SHARPENING PLATE

In this type of sanding accessory the backing disc is a flat circular metal face plate with a threaded spigot that screws in to the drill spindle socket. You remove the drill chuck in the normal way and fit the face plate in its place. However, while you can work freehand with the flexible backed sanding disc, you cannot do accurate work with the sanding plate unless you have it on a fixed mounting with a rigid support for the work. Both these items are available in the Black & Decker range of accessories. You fasten the horizontal drill stand on to your bench to hold the drill and sander and fit the disc sanding table on to it to form a solid support for the work (See under Horizontal Drill Stand). You can use a square to check the angle between the sanding table and the plate before tightening everything up.

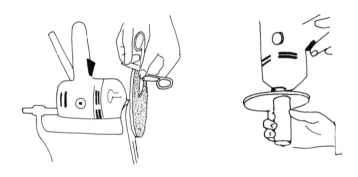

The Black & Decker metal sanding and sharpening plate is seen on left being used in the horizontal bench stand with the disc sanding table. On right the plate is being coated with adhesive cement before attaching the abrasive disc.

Before you can use the sander you have to attach the abrasive disc and with this type you stick it to the plate with a special adhesive, as follows:

1 Turn the plate by hand to make sure that it is not rubbing against the table.
2 Start the drill and press the end of a stick of disc cement against the centre of the face plate.
3 As the friction softens the cement, move the stick slowly across the plate until the whole surface is coated with a thin layer of tacky cement.
4 Stop the motor and press an abrasive disc firmly on to the surface of the plate. The sander is now ready for action.

You can now use the sander for a wide variety of jobs whenever you want to produce two flat surfaces meeting in a sharp edge and exactly at right angles. For instance you can clean up the sawn edge of a wooden plank or batten, sand across end grain or shape a radius, leaving the sanded face smooth and exactly at right angles. You can sand the mating faces of various joints knowing that the finished job will be square and the joints a good tight fit.

By using the mitre guide that comes with the table you can sand timber to any angle you please and repeat the process as often as you like. This is particularly useful when you are making up picture frames and similar articles where the mitred ends must be absolutely flat, square to the face of the frame and at exactly 45° to the length. When the abrasive disc gets clogged and useless you simply peel it off and stick another in its place.

Eventually the cement may need renewing and before doing this you must first remove the old cement. This is best done when the disc is cold—not at the end of a sanding session.

To remove the cement:

Peel off the old disc.

Start the drill.

Rest an old screwdriver on the table and, starting at the centre and working slowly out to the edge, let the point of the screwdriver slice away the cement, leaving the plate clean.

Apply a new coat of cement as above and stick a fresh abrasive disc on the plate.

As the table takes the full thrust of the abrasive surface on the work you are sanding, you will find that you can use the rigid disc sander with safety in shaping small wooden components held in your fingers.

USING THE PLATE FOR SHARPENING TOOLS

You can use the Metal Sanding and Sharpening Plate for sharpening things like workshop cutting tools—chisels, centre punches and so on as well as for knives, scissors and kitchen cutlery. The drill must of course be held in either the horizontal or vertical drill stand. For sharpening steel tools you should use a medium or fine grade aluminium oxide or emery sanding disc. If your drill is a 2-speed model, run it at its fast speed and keep the tool moving across the face of the disc as you grind it. Do not press on hard and from time to time stop to let the tool cool off. (Do not plunge it into water if you think you have let it get too hot.)

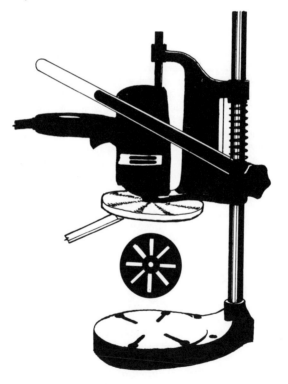

Power tool fitted with the metal sanding and sharpening plate being used in a vertical bench stand for sharpening tools. By cutting away the abrasive disc around the slots in the plate, the tool can be viewed through the back of the plate.

If you lack either the experience or the confidence to grind say, a carpenter's chisel correctly, here is a way to make the job easier:

1 Hold a sheet of abrasive in position on the plate and outline the shape of the slots from the back with a pencil.

2 Remove the abrasive disc and cut it away around the slot outlines with a pen knife.

3 Stick the abrasive disc on the plate with the cutaway parts coinciding with the slots in the plate.

4 Start the drill and look through the *back* of the plate as you grind the tool on the abrasive disc. You will see a dim but quite visible image of the tool which will make it easy for you to keep the tool at the correct angle to the surface of the abrasive disc.

You will find the above method helpful if you are a beginner, and it is a handy substitute for a grindstone if you do not possess one. However, you cannot grind as quickly this way as with a proper power grinder—e.g. the Black & Decker D 370 5 in.—and if you find yourself doing a lot of this work it would pay you to invest in the tool for the job.

SPECIAL ABRASIVE DISCS

For most power sanding jobs you use abrasive discs coated with either aluminium oxide or silicon oxide grains. Aluminium oxide has been chosen for the normal range of Black & Decker sanding discs because you can use aluminium oxide sanding paper on practically anything—wood, plastics, masonry or metal. But if you want to do a lot of work on metal, sharpening tools or smoothing off brazed or welded joints, you should buy discs coated with emery or better still, silicon oxide.

Nowadays, in addition to these standard materials you can buy a wide variety of abrasive discs, both flexible and rigid, coated with special abrasive materials—mostly extremely hard, coarse grits coated on paper, cloth or even thin sheet metal. The principal advantages of these discs are fast stock removal and long life. The ordinary abrasive sheets are consumable items that you throw away at the end of their limited life, but many of the special discs can be expected to stand up to years of hard use, so you only need to buy one. In any event it is a good idea to buy at least one to have handy when you run out of paper discs.

FINISHING SANDERS AND FINISHING SANDER ATTACHMENTS

A finishing sander is the tool to use for smoothing flat surfaces of woodwork ready for painting or for rubbing down already primed or undercoated surfaces before applying the next coat. This is the job that you normally do by rubbing the surface with a sheet of sandpaper folded around a block of wood and it is probably the most tedious and tiring part of any decorating programme. So naturally it is the part that gets the least attention or even none at all. And nine times out of ten it explains why an amateur paint job *looks* an amateur paint job.

The powered finishing sander takes all the effort out of sanding and rubbing down, does it far quicker and leaves a much smoother finish. It uses a standard sized sheet of abrasive paper stretched over a pressure plate covered with a layer of sponge rubber and covering an area roughly 7 in. X 3 5/8 in. or just over 25 sq. in. The motor housed in the body of the sander drives an eccentric gear giving a high speed rotary action to the pressure plate making the sheet of sandpaper move around rapidly in tiny circles over the surface being sanded. In fact every particle of abrasive in contact with the surface sands a circle about 3/16 in. diameter 4,000 times a minute. And as all the circles overlap you very quickly get a smooth surface ready for paint or any other type of finish. (Because of the circular movement of the sanding plate this tool is also known as an orbital sander.)

High spots in the surface are sanded from all angles so there is no tendency to leave hard ridges of grain standing while cutting away the softer wood between.

Various types and grades of abrasive sheet are made for the finishing sander and by using a suitable variety you can also smooth metal, plastics, laminates and plaster. (See Choosing The Right Abrasive Sheet, below.)

The Black & Decker finishing sander attachment turns any Black & Decker home user power tool into an orbital sander for preparing surfaces for painting.

THE BLACK & DECKER FINISHING SANDER ATTACHMENT

The finishing sander attachment is designed to turn any Black & Decker home user power drill into a finishing sander. The performance of the attachment is similar to that of the integral finishing sander and if your power tool budget is limited and you do not mind the inconvenience of changing over the drill chuck and the attachment, this could be your best buy.

The attachment comes to you in two parts: the body, holding the platen (the pressure plate over which you fasten the abrasive sheet) and the eccentric drive adaptor which couples the drill spindle to the platen and gives it its rotary movement.

The eccentric drive adaptor has a projecting boss which lies off the centre line of the drill spindle. This boss engages with a socket in the back of the platen when you fit the attachment. When you switch on the drill and the drive adaptor rotates, the platen follows the eccentric movement of the boss to impart the rotary scrubbing motion to the abrasive sheet. It can do this because it is fastened to the base of the attachment by four rubber pillars, one at each corner of the base.

93

HOW TO FIT THE ATTACHMENT

The attachment is coupled to the chuck spindle so before you can fit it you must first unscrew the chuck. Briefly, the way to do this is to point the drill away from you, insert the chuck key, turn it until it sticks out on the right of the chuck and give it a smart tap with a light hammer or block of wood. This loosens the chuck on its thread and you can then unscrew it by hand. (If you are in doubt, read the detailed description of this operation given on p 23.)

This is what you do to fit the attachment:

1 Screw the threaded part of the drive adaptor into the power drill in place of the chuck you have just removed.

2 Unscrew the large wing nut in the front of the attachment body (anticlockwise) as far as it will go.

3 Insert the nose of the drill in the opening in the top of the attachment body, fitting the round spigot on the drive adaptor into the hollow recess in the base of the attachment.

4 Turn the large wing nut clockwise so that the carriage on top of the attachment body slides towards the drill and the two claws on the front of the carriage enter the front slot in the drill gear case (the slot nearest the chuck).

5 Screw the wing nut home firmly but do not use force. See that the claws are properly entered in the slot.

6 The sanding attachment is now ready for use.

At each end of the platen there is a paper grip consisting of four sprockets formed on a shaft. By turning the shaft with a screwdriver in a slot at the end, you can draw in and anchor the sheet of sandpaper. The face of the platen is covered by a layer of rubber foam to provide a resilient backing for the abrasive sheet.

HOW TO FIT THE ABRASIVE SHEET

Some types of abrasive sheet are inclined to be difficult to fit because the bonding adhesive makes them too stiff to be easily threaded into the paper grip. You can get over this by drawing in the last couple of inches at each end over the edge of the work bench to break up the hard layer of adhesive. It also helps if you 'dog ear' the corners of the sheet at each end to form tapered shoulders. Now proceed:

1 Rest the tool with the pressure plate flat on the bench or table.

2 Insert one end of the sheet, abrasive side up, under the sprocket shaft at one end. Make sure that it is correctly lined up with the platen.

3 Insert a screwdriver in the slot in the end of the sprocket shaft and turn it to draw in about 1/2 in. of the sheet.

4 Fold the abrasive sheet around the face of the platen and insert it under the sprocket shaft at the other end of the platen.

5 Turn the sprocket shaft with a screwdriver to draw the sheet tight over the face of the platen. Unless the sheet is stretched tight it will not follow the movement of the platen and will have little or no sanding effect.

Sprocket shafts at each end of the platen grip the abrasive sheet and hold it in position. The shafts are turned with a screwdriver to draw in the sheet and stretch it tightly over the face of the platen.

CHOOSING THE RIGHT ABRASIVE SHEET

Before you start using your finishing sander, make sure you have the right type and grade of paper. Ordinary sandpaper is not suitable. The grains of abrasive on this type of paper are close together because they have to make up in numbers what they lack in resistance to wear. This is all very well for hand sanding where you only remove small amounts of the surface with a lot of rubbing. But a power sander smooths down the surface so quickly that ordinary close-grained sandpaper would soon clog and stop cutting. So the special type of abrasive paper made for power sanding is quite different from ordinary sandpaper in two important ways: it is coated with grains of aluminium oxide, a man-made abrasive very much harder than even the hardest natural abrasive, and the grains are more widely separated, leaving plenty of room for the sanding dust to collect and allowing it to fall away when the sander is lifted off the surface. In addition it is coated on a tougher backing which is less likely to tear than ordinary sandpaper. You will now see the benefit of buying the proper abrasive sheet for your finishing sander. The right material costs a little more but it is much cheaper in the long run than bargain packets of ordinary sandpaper offered at half the price. The grade of abrasive used ranges from 36 grit—the coarsest corresponding roughly to No. 3 glasspaper—to 150 grit, the finest normally required for woodwork and corresponding to No. 0 glasspaper.

Ordinary close coated sandpaper (left) used in a finishing sander soon clogs and becomes useless. Modern open coated papers allow the dust particles to fall clear so that the abrasive can keep on cutting.

Most of the time you want a finishing sander for woodwork for which you can buy abrasive sheet in fine (150 grit), medium (100 grit), coarse (60 grit) and extra coarse (36 grit). But you can also buy special grades and other abrasives for use on other materials, including masonry, and there are several grades of emery coated sheet for smoothing steel and other metals.

HOW TO USE THE FINISHING SANDER ATTACHMENT

You use the finishing sander by simply holding it flat against the surface of the work and pressing the trigger switch to start the motor running. When you do this the tool vibrates at high speed and as you move it over the surface it will leave a trail of dust behind, showing that the abrasive sheet is rubbing down the high spots. There is no need to press hard on the tool, its own weight will be enough on a horizontal surface and if you have to sand a wall or a ceiling it is only necessary to apply enough pressure to keep the abrasive sheet in firm contact with the surface. Any extra pressure merely sands off material faster than the dust can escape. The result is that the sheet becomes clogged and less and less able to do its job properly.

The sander rubs in tiny circles and the scrubbing action acts in all directions with and across the grain. So there is no need for you to work to any particular pattern (as there is with a flexible disc sander); you just move it over the surface irrespective of the shape of the work or the direction of the grain.

The grade of abrasive sheet you choose will depend on the state of the original surface and the final finish you want to produce. When smoothing sawn or roughly finished timber or old and flaking paint work you should go over it once or twice with a coarse or very coarse abrasive and follow up with the next finer grade up to the finest if you want a silky-smooth finish. The coarse grade abrasive will get rid of the initial roughness quickly but if you look closely at the surface you will see that it is covered with fine circular scratches. You use the next finer grade to smooth away these scratches, but you will still be able to see more although they will be finer and shallower than before. When you get rid of these with finer and finer abrasive sheets, the scratches left by the last abrasive will be invisible to the naked eye and the surface will then be ready for painting, varnishing or polishing.

There is no need to use a coarse abrasive if the surface is in reasonably good condition to start with—e.g. planed timber, existing paintwork that you want to go over with a different colour, or primer or undercoating on timber that has already been sanded smooth. For these surfaces a medium or fine abrasive is all you need.

If you want a really first class finish it is a good idea to wet the surface after the final sanding, allow it to dry, and then sand it again. The water 'raises the grain' and the second sanding operation gets rid of the fuzz of projecting fibres.

The scope of the finishing sander is not restricted to plain, flat surfaces. You can use it around curves and mouldings and in places where you can only get part of the abrasive surface into contact with the surface—e.g. a strip along the front edge or down the side. When you use it this way, however, you have to remember that your normal pressure is concentrated on a small area and the abrasive action is proportionately more severe. So you have to watch that you do not press on too hard or too long or you will remove more of the surface than you intend.

This point is specially important in dealing with corners when the pressure is concentrated on a thin edge. If you are sanding down an undercoated surface for instance, the sander will very quickly cut through to the raw timber in going round a sharp edge or along a line of moulding. If you are starting from scratch with new timber it is a good idea to use the sander to round off any sharp edges before you start, then there will not be the risk of cutting through the subsequent coats of paint when you are sanding in preparation for the finishing coat.

The extra abrasion you get when you concentrate the action of the sander on a small area comes in useful when you are sanding a surface with an odd bad patch here and there, you can tilt the sander forward so that only the front edge bears on the bad spot. When you do this, the abrasive will work faster but do not forget that it will also wear out quicker. So if you want to scrub away a patch of rust, for instance. use a wire brush, preferably one mounted in a power drill (p 139).

97

THE BLACK & DECKER INTEGRAL POWER FINISHING SANDER

The Black & Decker finishing sander is powered by a motor housed in a moulded case with an integral pistol grip handle fitted with an on-off trigger switch. A second moulded handle with a large, easy-grip knob can be screwed into either side of the alloy case, so the sander can be controlled by both hands with a right or left hold.

The housing for the gearbox and the platen drive is integral with the motor casing and encloses resilient supports at each corner to which the platen is screwed. An eccentric boss on the end of the drive fits into a bearing fastened to the back of the platen so that when the drive shaft turns, the platen follows the movement of the eccentric and produces the required rotary scrubbing action. The resilience of the four rubber supports allows the pressure plate the necessary freedom to rotate in this way.

The Black & Decker integral power finishing sander is identical in performance to the finishing sander attachment with the added convenience of an integral tool that is always ready for use.

The 3-core mains cable enters the casing through the pistol grip handle as in the power drills. The trigger switch can be locked in the 'on' position by pressing in the button on the side of the handle while holding the trigger pressed down. The trigger stays locked down until you release it by pressing it again.

The tool must be connected to a power point through a 3-pin plug, providing a reliable earth connexion. As with the other workshop power tools it is best to fit a rubber or resilient plastic plug that will not break if you drop it on a hard surface.

The method of fitting the abrasive sheet and the operation of the sander in all other respects are identical with those already described for the power drill and finishing sander attachment. Here again, if the limits of your budget and your bench and cupboard space allow, there are obvious advantages in buying the tool for the job instead of having to put your power drill out of commission while you use it to drive the attachment. Do not forget that if you do a lot of making and mending in your workshop and rely on a single power unit for everything, it will naturally need more frequent maintenance and all your operations will be held up while it is away being serviced.

OTHER TYPES OF SANDER

There is no single type of sander that will do all the jobs you are likely to want to do but the basic sanders described above will do most of them. However, there are other types that you might find useful for specialised jobs that come up from time to time.

DRUM SANDERS

These are useful for following narrow edges with curves in them— like the edge of a free-shaped coffee table top or the inside of a hand-hold opening in a wooden panel. Their great merit is that they can be used along the grain of the wood even if the drum moves across the grain.

Abrasive drum sanders offer an alternative for special jobs - e.g. sanding curved edges. Several layers of abrasive paper are mounted on a resilient plastic foam drum. Used layers can be peeled off to expose fresh abrasive.

99

This type of sander has a resilient plastic foam cylinder mounted on an arbor that you can grip in the chuck of your power drill. The abrasive material is in the form of a long strip coiled up to make a band which fits on to the foam cylinder. When you start up the drill the cylinder spins round and you can then press the abrasive band against the edge to be sanded. Eventually the outside of the band gets worn and clogged but when this happens you just peel off the outer layer, expose a fresh lot of abrasive and get on with the job.

Drum sanders are made in a wide range of diameters and widths. The Black & Decker abrasive kit provides a choice of useful sizes. You can buy larger sizes than those in the kit but you have to remember that the larger the diameter and width of the band, the more power it takes to drive it and the greater the risk of overloading the power drill.

METAL DISC SANDERS

One is available which is mounted on a universal joint so that you can sand flat surfaces with no risk of cutting grooves with the edge even when the drill is tilted at an angle. The cutting face on this disc is made of thin steel with sharp-edged perforations something like those in the type of grater used in the kitchen for shredding vegetables. As the teeth do not clog, it makes a useful tool for cleaning off thick layers of old paint ahead of the finishing sander, flattening down plaster and fillers and general stock removal operations on wood, plastics, asbestos and similar materials.

BELT SANDERS

Some manufacturers offer a belt sander attachment in which a wide belt of abrasive sheet passes around a pair of drums, one of which is driven by the power tool. This type of sander has a number of specialised applications in industry, but it needs more power to drive it effectively than the normal home user's power tool can provide. As a result such attachments tend to be more expensive and not as generally useful as the disc and orbital types.

One of the many types of special abrasive disc for use with power tools. This one is made of perforated metal and has a universal joint which allows the disc to tilt to suit the angle of the surface.

DRILL STANDS

There are two types of stand—vertical and horizontal—which you can use to extend the scope of your power drill by turning it into a bench-mounted machine tool.

With the vertical stand, rest or fix the work on the base plate and bring the drill down on to it with a hand lever. The principal purpose of this stand is to make it easy to drill holes accurately although with the drill held in the vertical position some of the chuck-mounted accessories are easier to manage too.

In a horizontal drill stand the drill becomes a different kind of tool that you use less for drilling than as a fixed source of power for driving things like rotary sanders and abrasive discs of all kinds, polishing buffs and bonnets, wire brushes and grinding wheels so that you can have both hands free to manipulate the work. By adding a sanding table you can extend its scope still further for grinding, sanding and shaping with an accuracy impossible with free-hand working.

Black & Decker accessories of this type are described below.

THE BLACK & DECKER VERTICAL DRILL STAND

The vertical drill stand converts any of the home user range of Black & Decker power drills into a bench drilling machine. This arrangement has a number of advantages that you miss when you can only use the power tool for freehand drilling:

1 It drills holes which are automatically at right angles to the base.
2 In conjunction with a jig secured to the base it can be used for accurate repetition work.
3 It gives positive control of the drill feed, prevents snatching on breakthrough and reduces the risk of breaking small diameter drills.
4 It lets you set the depth of the hole accurately and drill any number of holes to the same depth without further adjustment.
5 It frees both hands for manipulating work being sanded, ground, wire brushed or polished.

6 It leaves the bench top clear and provides a safer parking place for the drill when it is not being used.

The Black & Decker vertical drill stand consists of three principal items: (a) a base which has slots for clamping bolts and a collar and clamping bolt for the stand pillar, (b) the tubular steel stand pillar and (c) the drill carriage. You bolt the base either on to the bench top or if bench space is limited, on to a stout slab of timber which you can clamp to the bench when you want to use the drill stand. The pillar, which is supplied with the drill carriage already fitted, drops into the collar in the base plate and is fixed by the clamping bolt. The power drill is held in the carriage between a yoke at the lower end and a fixing bolt which screws through the back lug of the carriage and engages the recess in the back of the drill case. The

In a vertical drill stand the power tool can only move up and down at right angles to the base plate. This makes it easy to drill straight, accurate holes just where you want them. The slots in the base plate let you bolt the job down securely or hold a fixed jig for repetition work.

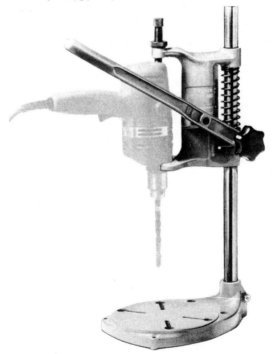

fixing bolt is secured by a lock nut. The carriage, normally held in the raised position by a return spring, can be lowered by a pivoted hand lever to feed the drill into the work. A clamping bolt tightened by a large hand-size moulded knob, locks the carriage anywhere on the pillar and can be used to adjust the height of the carriage to suit the work and also the lower limit of travel of the drill, i.e. the depth of the hole.

HOW TO USE THE DRILL STAND

The important feature of the drill stand is that it holds everything rigid—the drill, the base and the work. So be sure before you start that the drill is secure in the carriage with the recesses on the front of the gearcase engaging the tips of the yoke and the fixing bolt screwed up and secured with the lock nut. (You have the lock nut below the lug on the carriage for all single speed drills except the D 900 and above the lug for the D 900 and all 2-speed drills.) Next be sure that the base is screwed or clamped solidly to the bench top.

Finally make sure the work is fastened firmly to the base of the drill stand. How you do this will depend on the shape of the work and whether there are any existing holes or projections to take bolts or clamps. If you are doing a one-off job it will not matter if the holding down arrangements are a bit primitive, but if you want to do repetition work then it will be worthwhile for you to work out an efficient quick-release clamp. However, you will usually be able to manage with one of the various job clamping arrangements described under How To Hold It (p 106).

When you want to take the drill right through material clamped directly on to the base plate make sure that the drill is over the centre hole in the base plate and that the depth is set so that the drill does not go right through into the bench. However, if you have backed up the job with a piece of scrap to prevent the drill from splintering or tearing as it breaks through then you will have to set the depth so that the full width of the drill just enters the scrap.

Once you have locked the pillar with the clamp in the base plate you can adjust the height, penetration and position of the drill by slacking off the big moulded knob that locks the drill carriage and swinging the drill anywhere in a circle around the pillar. This is useful because some things are easier to manage flat on the bench at the back of the drill than on the raised base of the stand. Always slacken the clamp bolt gradually; you do not want the carriage to slip and bang the drill down on the base plate.

Wipe a film of light oil over the bright metal of the pillar to protect it from rust and let the carriage slide freely. But if you do any work with abrasive discs, the loose grit thrown off will stick to the oil on the pillar and form a highly efficient grinding paste. So before you go in for any sanding or grinding, put a protective wrapping of paper around the pillar.

THE BLACK & DECKER HORIZONTAL DRILL STAND

The Black & Decker horizontal drill stand is designed to hold any of the home user drills. It is a rigid carriage with holes in the flange to take screws or bolts for fixing it to the bench. As in the vertical stand carriage and the headstock or the lathe attachment, the front end of the drill is located in a yoke which engages with recesses in the gear case on each side of the chuck. A screw through the back of the stand fits into the circular recess in the back of the drill casing and is secured by a lock nut. (The original pressed steel horizontal drill stand is being superseded by an alloy diecast stand which is in fact identical with the carriage that forms the headstock of the lathe attachment.)

A horizontal bench stand turns your power tool into a fixed power unit for grinding, polishing and wire brushing with both hands free to manipulate the work.

With your power drill fixed in the horizontal drill stand you can use it to drive all the Black & Decker sanding, wire brushing, buffing and polishing accessories. In fact, so long as the stand is firmly screwed or clamped to the bench, this is the most convenient way of using these accessories to work on objects that you can bring to the drill. It leaves both your hands free to manipulate the article and by choosing the right accessories you can do freehand sanding or wire brushing, polishing, grinding and sharpening.

You can remove the chuck and screw in a 3 in. wire cup brush, a rubber backing pad for sanding or a metal sanding and sharpening plate. If you do not want to remove the chuck you can use it to hold the alternative rubber backing pad fitted with a 1/4 in. chuck shank.

You can fit the Black & Decker wheel arbor in the chuck and use it to drive a 3 in. general purpose grinding wheel or a 4 in. wire wheel brush. And for polishing you can fit a 3 in. rag buff to the arbor or even use the car polishing bonnet fitted over the rubber backing pad.

DISC SANDING TABLE

By adding the Black & Decker disc sanding table to the horizontal drill stand you finish up with a useful bench tool that will do accurate disc sanding of wood and plastics articles and can also be used for sharpening tools as described under Rigid Disc Sanders.

The sanding table is intended for use with the Black & Decker Metal Sanding and Sharpening Plate. It fits on to the front of the horizontal stand and is held by two hook bolts and wing nuts. A wing nut on the underside of the table lets you set the table parallel to the sanding plate. (You should always set the table so that it is just clear of the plate; it is dangerous to have a gap between the edge of the table and the plate where small objects might get wedged.)

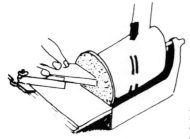

By adding a sanding table to the horizontal drill stand and using a suitable abrasive disc on the metal sanding and sharpening plate you can carry out accurate sanding and mitring operations on wood or metal.

The adjustable mitre gauge which slides in a groove along the outside edge of the table lets you sand or grind accurate mitres at any angle from 30° to 90°.

The disc sanding table for the superseded pressed steel horizontal drill stand is not suitable for fixing to the current die cast alloy stand. If you should be sold the wrong type of sanding table in error your Black & Decker supplier will exchange it for the correct type to fit your horizontal drill stand model.

HOW TO HOLD IT

When you are working with hand tools you can afford to take chances on how you hold the work, but with power tools you must fix it solidly if you want to do a good job and do it safely. So job clamping arrangements are as important as the tool itself. Any money you spend on clamps or fixing devices is wisely invested.

There are one or two traditional fixing aids that you ought to have in your kit as a matter of course. First of these is the familiar C-clamp, shaped like a C with a wing bolt screwed through one side of the gap and tightening against a flat on the opposite side. Clamps like this will either hold two parts together while you drill them or glue one to the other or you can use them to fasten a clamp or board to the bench so that you can drill or saw it. It is worth while buying one or two different sizes so that you can hold anything from thin sheets of material up to at least 3 in. thickness.

Next there is the bench hold fast type of clamp. This is an adjustable arm on the end of a serrated bar which drops into a steel bush let into the top of the bench. When you tighten the screw that presses the arm down on top of the work the serrated bar locks in the bush. As you go on turning the screw the pressure of the arm increases and clamps the work firmly to the top of the bench. To release the holdfast you simply slacken the screw off a turn or so and this automatically loosens the bar in the bush.

The device acts as a quick release clamp that is instantly adjustable over a wide range of sizes. The place to fit a clamp of this type is near the edge of the bench so that you can use it for holding timber that you want to saw over the edge of the bench; for instance, if you want to do some jigsawing which requires constant shifting of the wood to prevent the saw from cutting into the edge of the bench.

Then apart from regular clamps it is useful to have an assortment of bolts and odd pieces of steel strip for making up your own clamps and particularly for fastening work down on to the base plate of the

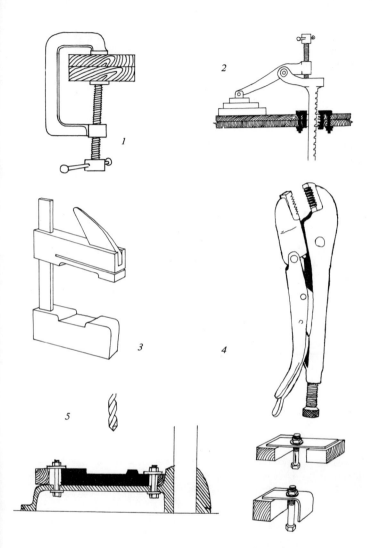

Practically every power tool operation is easier when the work is firmly clamped to a solid support. Here are the many clamps you will find useful. 1 – G - clamp, 2 – bench holdfast, 3 – the Black & Decker quick grip clamp, 4 – quick release adjustable wrench, 5 – improvised clamps for holding work on the base plate of the vertical drill stand.

Black & Decker vertical drill stand. There are slots in the base of the stand and each slot has a hole at one end to let you drop the head of the clamping bolt through. If you use ordinary hexagon headed bolts you will not be able to stop the bolt from turning when you tighten the nut down on to the clamping bar. But if you use standard 1/4 in. Whitworth coach bolts, the squared neck fits into the slot and stops the bolt from turning. (You may have to file a little off the flats if they are too wide for the slot.)

You can clamp the work on to the base of the drill stand by passing the clamping bolt through a strip of steel with one end resting on the work and the other on a piece of packing to keep it level. Or, if you are dealing with one thickness of material you can bend one side of the steel strip at right angles to form a support of the right height and dispense with the loose piece of packing.

THE BLACK & DECKER QUICK GRIP CLAMP

The Black & Decker quick grip clamp will do most of the jobs that a G-clamp will do and in addition it is operated by a quick release lever. The jaws are faced with cork so that it will not scratch the surface of the work it is holding and as the pressure is spread over a much greater area than with a G-clamp it does not leave dents behind.

The clamp consists of a wooden pillar with one fixed and one adjustable jaw which is normally free to slide on the pillar but jams automatically when the movable jaw is tightened down to the job by the operating lever.

In addition to its use for securing the work being drilled or sawn, the clamp is ideal for holding down power tool equipment that has been mounted on an independent base so that it can be cleared off the bench when it is not being used.

You need to be specially careful about your clamping arrangements when you are drilling sheet metal because the sudden shock that occurs when the drill breaks through could free the metal and spin it around with the drill. Always fix a stop to the bench or the drill stand to prevent the sheet metal from turning if the clamp slips.

WOOD TURNING ATTACHMENTS

More and more handymen, do-it-yourself enthusiasts and early retirers (from business—not to bed) are taking up wood turning as a hobby. It has a lot to recommend it; probably its chief appeal is that it is a satisfying outlet for most of us who suffer from an artistic urge without the ability to express it. The creative thrill of shaping a piece of wood in the lathe is its own reward but do not forget that as you are enjoying the sensation you can also be turning out pleasing and useful objects that make acceptable presents or can even bring you in a useful cash bonus from your local gift shop or hardware store.

If you like, you can pay a hundred pounds for a wood turning lathe but for a tenth of that sum you can buy a lathe attachment plus the power drill to drive it that will keep you happy for years before you want to graduate to something more sophisticated.

Most of the leading power tool manufacturers make a lathe attachment for their own electric drills. The principle is the same for all makes. You have a lathe bed in the form of a rail or pair of rails with a holder (the headstock) for the power tool fixed at one end. The wood to be turned is held between two steel centres, one on the drill spindle and the other on a sliding saddle (the tailstock) which can be locked anywhere along the bed. The driving centre on the drill spindle has a sharp edged fork which digs into the end of the wood so that it turns with the drill spindle. The tailstock centre is a plain point that acts as a bearing to support the spinning workpiece. Between the two centres the bed carries a horizontal bar (the tool rest) which can be adjusted to the correct height and position to support the gouge or chisel used for turning the wood.

When you are using your drill in the Black & Decker lathe attachment you remove the chuck (p 23) and screw either the driving centre or face plate into the spindle in its place, depending on the type of turning you are going to do. Both items are supplied with the lathe attachment. A special internal turning attachment is also supplied. This attachment is for turning articles like egg cups which are too small to be worked on the face plate.

In addition to the lathe attachment and power drill you will need a set of wood turning tools. You should be able to buy the right sort of thing where you buy the lathe attachment or at any good tool shop. A simple selection of four tools will be all you need for a long time, later as you become more expert, you can buy others or make your own for turning special shapes. To start with, ask for two gouges—1 in. and 1/4 in. across, a 1 in. chisel and a parting tool. The big gouge is for turning the wood quickly down to within 1/8 in. or so of the finished shape; the 1/4 in. gouge for turning details and working the inside of bowl shapes; the chisel to follow up the big gouge and finish the surface smoothly down to size and finally the parting tool for severing the article you have turned from the waste wood at each end.

As you buy these tools the ends are ground to the correct shape but they still require sharpening to a keen cutting edge with an oilstone. The chapter on Bench Grinders tells you how to do this. Remember successful wood turning is impossible unless your tools are really sharp and have the special type of edge needed for wood turning. Ordinary woodworking chisels and gouges have their own sort of edge which is quite useless for turning. So either turn to the chapter on Sharpening Tools or get somebody with experience in wood turning to show you how before you start.

The method of turning outlined above is called turning between centres and is used for long shapes like lamp standards, chair legs and candlesticks that need supporting at both ends. In addition to this method lathe attachments are usually equipped for another method called face plate work in which the wood to be turned is fastened to a circular plate which you mount on the end of the drill spindle in place of the driving centre. In this method the wood is held at one side only and as there is no tailstock support to get in the way, you can shape the front as well as the rim of the work. This is the method you use for turning bowls, platters, lampstand bases, boxes and lids and so on.

If you can spare the space on your workbench you can screw the lathe bed on to the top and leave it there, but if you are short of space, you can fix it to a sturdy plank which you can fasten on the top of the bench with a pair of clamps (p 106) when you want to use it.

Although all lathe attachments work on the same principle, they must be used with the drill they were designed for; you cannot use a drill made by one manufacturer to drive a lathe attachment made by another. The important things you want to know about a lathe attachment are the length of the longest piece of wood it will turn between centres and the diameter of the biggest piece it will turn both between centres and on the face plate.

THE BLACK & DECKER LATHE ATTACHMENT

The bed of the Black & Decker lathe attachment is a steel channel shaped to form two parallel rails. Bolt the drill carriage, the tool rest and the tailstock to these rails. The drill is secured in a three-point mounting in the same way as in the horizontal and vertical drill stands. Projections on a U-shaped yoke on the front of the drill carriage engage with recesses on each side of the drill gear casing. The drill is held in position by a 7/8 in. bolt screwed through the back of the carriage into the recess in the back of the drill case. The position of the drill carriage is fixed at the extreme left of the bed but you can adjust the position of both the tool rest and the tailstock to suit the work in hand.

The Black & Decker lathe attachment screws to the bench top and turns your power tool into a lathe for both face plate and between-centres turning.

HOW TO TURN BETWEEN CENTRES
For your first attempts, start with a length of wood that is already round: 1 ft cut off an old broom handle or an old wooden curtain rod would be just the thing. Make sure the ends are square and flat and then use a pair of compasses to find the exact centre of each end. Knock a centre punch into the centre to leave a conical pit.

Now drill a hole either in the top of your bench or a piece of scrap hardwood just big enough to take the screw end of the driving centre. Stand the driving centre upright in this hole and place the centre punch mark on one end of the wood on the point of the driving centre. Tap the wood with a mallet to drive in the point of the centre until the knife-edged projections bite into the wood. Do this with both ends of the wood and put a dab of furniture wax or candle grease in each centre hole just in case you want to change ends later.

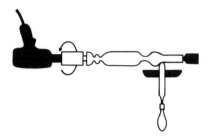

When turning between centres the work is held between the driving and tailstock centres. It is shaped by cutting or scraping with a tool supported on the tool rest.

Now screw the driving centre *complete with its fibre washer* into the drill spindle, slack off the tailstock and slide it along until you can support the prepared wood between the centres, making sure that the projections on the driving centre engage with the marks on either side of the centre. Lock the tailstock on the bed with the holding-down bolt and move the screw adjustment on the tailstock centre in or out with the tommy bar supplied with the lathe attachment until you can just turn the wood by hand. Then tighten the lock nut on the screw adjustment while you hold the centre with the tommy bar.

Finally adjust the tool rest so that it lies parallel with the wood and about 1/4 in. to 1/2 in. away from it with the top about 1/8 in. to 1/16 in. below the centre line. So much for the job, now for the tools.

There are two ways of shaping wood in a lathe, just as there are two ways of dealing with the skin on a potato. Just as you can peel a potato or scrape it, you can peel wood or scrape it to the shape you want.

The peeling action calls for a thin, sharp blade held almost flat against the surface and you adjust the thickness of the peeling by very slight changes in the angle of the blade while you steady it by pressing the flat of the blade against the surface. Peeling this way calls for an accurate adjustment of the blade angle but the actual cutting takes very little effort.

There are two ways of shaping wood in the lathe: Scraping, (left) is easier for beginners. Cutting (right) requires more skill and a very sharp tool.

The scraping action drags the sharp edge over the surface at right angles and a thin blade would soon get its edge rubbed off. For scraping you need a strong edge with an angle of around 90° between the two faces. The action calls for very little skill as quite big changes in the angle of the blade or in the pressure you put on the surface make very little difference to the result. But it is harder work and you do not get anything like the smooth finish produced by peeling off shavings.

When you are an expert at wood turning you will be a peeler and do most of your work with cutting tools ground to a fine edge, but as a beginner, especially if you have no expert to guide you, you will be safer to start by scraping. For your first efforts use a scraping tool with a rounded point. (See Sharpening Tools, p 126.) The handle of the tool should be at least 9 in. long and securely fitted.

Check that the work is free to turn, then press the switch on the drill handle and lock it on. Now position the turning tool so that it lies flat on the rest, holding the end of the handle in your right hand and steadying the tool against the rest with the other.

You are now ready to start turning and this is how you do it: Raise your right hand so that the tool points slightly downwards. Slide the tool forward on the rest until the tip of the cutting edge is just below the centre of the wood; it must be so close to the wood that when you lower your right hand the edge of the tool will make contact with the wood. As you do this, the edge will scrape a groove in the wood. You have now started turning.

You can now practise by letting the tool slide sideways along the rest to widen the groove or pushing it forwards to deepen the groove. The power and speed of the lathe make it possible for you to cut away wood at a fast rate and so long as you keep the cutting edge of the tool just on or below the centre you will not have any trouble in controlling it.

This way, as the wood presses down on the cutting edge, it can only push it further away and make it take a lighter cut. But if the edge of the tool is cutting above the centre line, then the downward

113

pressure of the wood tends to make the edge dig in deeper and deeper. Result: the tool jerks out of your hand or the wood breaks or jumps out of the centres, or, if you are very unlucky, the end of the tool snaps off.

So, bearing this in mind, experiment with the tool held flat, then at an angle, moving it to left or right and noting how the wood cuts in each case. Try raising and lowering your right hand to control the rate of cutting and try moving it in the arc of a circle, pivoted on the rest. Make a point of keeping the scraping edge of the tool moving otherwise the friction set up by the wood rubbing against the edge may overheat it and draw the temper. The tool will then quickly loose its keen edge.

Turning something that is already round is the easiest way to start, but mostly you will be working with sawn timber which will have a square section. So practise next on a 6 in. to 12 in. long blank ripsawn off a piece of 1 1/2 in. to 2 in. board, cutting a piece as wide as the board is thick. Draw diagonals across each end and knock the driving centre into the wood at the intersections of the lines.

You can now set up the blank between the centres of your lathe and adjust the tool rest so that it is just clear of the corners of the blank as they turn. The rough turning job is easier if you first plane off the corners to leave an octagonal section. If you have a 2-speed drill you can set it at low speed and turn the corners off the blank if you do not mind the heavy vibration at the start, but you will have to stop later and move the tool rest closer to the job for your finishing cuts and you must remember to tighten up the tailstock centre at the same time because the centre holes are sure to be enlarged by the hammering of the tool on the corners.

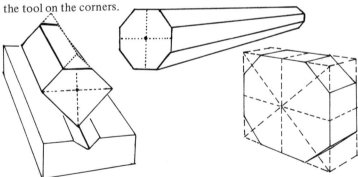

Left: Turning square stock between centres is easier if you first plane off the corners. Make the holder illustrated for repetition work. Right: Slabs for face plate turning can be roughed to shape by sawing off the corners.

HOW TO TURN ON THE FACE PLATE

When you feel quite at home with the scraping tool working between centres, try your hand with the face plate. For this you need a blank of flat wood up to 2 in. thick and big enough to let you mark out a circle on it from 3 in. to 4 in. across. Cut away the surplus wood with a saw and then place the faceplate on the blank, face downwards, and fix it in position with four short screws. Now screw the faceplate in to the drill spindle in place of the driving centre and adjust the tool rest so that it is just clear of the corners of the blank when you turn the faceplate by hand.

If you have a 2-speed drill you should engage the lower speed for turning anything bigger than 1 1/2 in. diameter, which includes most faceplate work. Practise with the scraping tool, first work on the edge to get rid of the corners and then, with the tool rest turned parallel to the front face, try hollowing out a rough bowl. Control the cutting edge of the tool by swinging your right hand in an arc, up or down to control the depth of your cut and from side to side to increase the width. When you want to make a long cut parallel to the rest, do not try to do it by sliding the tool along the rest. Instead, build it up in a series of shallow curves to leave a slightly wavy surface which you can finish flat in one continuous light cut.

Up to now you have been working with scraping tools which can be curved, pointed or flat ended or anything in between. In fact if you want to run off several dozen identical items, e.g. a set of draughts, you can make your own tools to do the tricky details in one go by grinding the end of an old flat file to the exact shape you want.

By keeping your scraping tools sharp, you can get a finish on hardwood which will need only a rub with fine glass paper and a spot of wax polish to look really professional. You can do both the glasspapering and polishing in the lathe. This saves time and makes a better looking job. Back up the glass paper with a pad of soft cloth (not your fingers), and keep it moving across the surface to avoid scoring it.

There are all sorts of ways of finishing and you can find them out for yourself from any book on woodworking. But if you want a quick finish for natural wood, spin the wood in the lathe, press a piece of wax candle against it and let the friction melt the candle wax and make it flow over the surface. Follow up by holding a pad of cloth against the surface to add the final polish and take up the surplus wax.

USING THE CUTTING TOOLS

Scraping is one way of getting a smooth finish and it is a safe way of making a start, but it is too slow for cutting away large amounts of surplus wood and even as a finishing operation it tends to tear off the wood fibres instead of peeling or shaving them off. A real wood turner does most of his work with a cutting tool that has a knife edge. In the chisels the knife edge is straight and in the gouges it is curved. The edge of the chisel is ground on both faces but the edge of the gouge is ground on the outside curve only. You can buy wood turning chisels with the edge ground either straight across or on the skew. Gouges are ground with the edge straight across with square shoulders or the shoulders may be ground back to make a round nosed tool.

Then there is a third type of cutting tool made like a chisel with a deep, narrow blade about 1/4 in. wide. This is the parting off tool and it is used for slicing a thin slot straight through the turned wood to cut it off clean and square. This is easier and more accurate than sawing. You may leave a small stem at the centre of the parted slot to finish off with a saw if you do not want to sever it completely in the lathe.

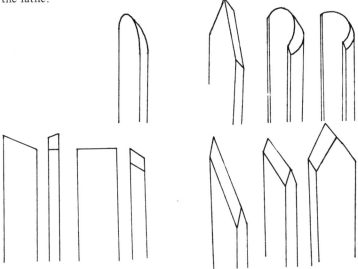

Wood turning tools are designed either for shaping by scraping (left) or cutting (right). Scraping tools can be made by grinding the ends of old files to the shape you want. It pays to buy cutting tools as these need careful forging, grinding and tempering.

Broadly speaking, you use the gouges for quickly turning the wood almost to size, and the chisels for finishing. Start with a length of wood between centres as you did for your scraping experiments and take a 1 in. gouge ground straight across with square shoulders. Adjust the tool rest at about centre height and as close to the wood as it will go without touching it.

Now try this before you switch on the lathe: hold the gouge on the rest, hollow side up, but this time instead of pointing it down slightly like a scraping tool, lower your right hand to raise the cutting edge until the bevel, not the edge, is resting against the wood. Look at it from the side and watch what happens when you turn the gouge either way. You will see that there is a point where the corner of the cutting edge of the gouge comes into contact with the wood. Notice that although the corner is ready to cut into the wood, the bevel is still resting on the surface. As long as the bevel stays in that position, the corner of the gouge will not dig in. Once you see that, you know the secret of using the cutting tools. Whether you are working with a gouge or a chisel, always keep the bevel rubbing against the wood you are turning and the tool will not play any tricks.

When turning with a cutting tool the bevel must rub against the work to prevent the edge from digging in. Top: Cut from right to left with the left hand corner of the gouge and left to right with the right hand corner. Bottom: Use only the bottom half of the cutting edge of the chisel (shaded).

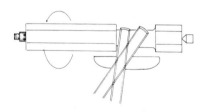

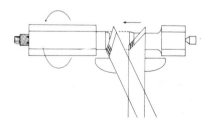

Now try the same exercise with the lathe running. Start by slanting the tool upwards from the rest so that the bevel is rubbing against the wood. Now slowly turn the gouge on to its left side and lift your right hand until the shoulder on the edge of the gouge starts to cut a groove in the wood. Swing the handle of the gouge to the right and the tool will move to the left and widen the groove you have just made. Turn the gouge so that the hollow of the curve looks to the right instead of the left and you can now make it cut in the opposite direction by swinging the handle to the left. With these basic movements of the gouge you can turn every possible shape in the lathe, but you will not produce a high quality finish. For this you have to use the chisel.

With the chisel, as with the gouge, the same rule applies: keep the bevel of the tool rubbing and you will have no trouble.

Now you are ready to use the chisel to smooth the piece of wood you have just roughed out with the gouge. Start as before with the chisel resting flat on the rest and sloping upwards so that the bevel of the tool rubs high up on the wood well away from either end. The cutting edge of the chisel should lie at an angle to the centre line of the wood. If it is ground on the skew this will automatically be taken care of, but if it is ground square you will have to swing the handle to one side to present the edge at an angle.

Now turn the chisel and at the same time raise the handle if necessary to bring the lower part of the cutting edge into contact with the wood. Try not to get the point of contact higher than half way up the edge and above all do not let the point on the high side of the edge touch the wood or it will dig in. (Now you can see the sense in using a really wide chisel that gives you plenty of edge to work with.)

The lower part of the edge of the chisel will now be planing off a light shaving with the bevel resting on the wood, burnishing it and preventing the edge from digging in. You can continue cutting by either sliding the tool along the rest towards the cutting edge, or swinging the handle in the opposite direction. In practice you do a bit of both, and the result is a smooth, level finish. In fact, so long as the edge of the tool is really sharp and you take a slow, fine cut, you will not need to finish it with glass paper.

WORKING ON THE FACEPLATE

The same rules apply to turning the outside of an article on the face plate: rough almost to size with the gouge and finish with the chisel. However, when you come to finish the inside of something like a bowl or a box, you will have to use a rounded scraping tool for finishing because the corners of the chisel would dig in. For the same reason, the gouge you use for roughing out the inside surfaces must have a rounded cutting edge without the square shoulders you get in a gouge which is ground straight across.

There is another special point about turning hollow articles. Most turning can be done from in front of the lathe, i.e. with the headstock on your left and the tailstock on your right. But when you want to work on the inside of a hollow the tool has to enter from the back, and to see what is going on you would have to lean across the bed which is dangerous because your tie or a loose part of your clothing could easily get caught up and pulled in by the revolving wood. Instead go around to the other side of the lathe (or turn it around on the bench) and work from the back with the tool rest suitably adjusted to support the tool from that angle.

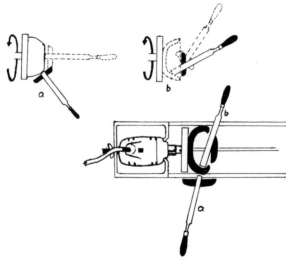

Most turning can be done from the front of the lathe (a) but when turning a bowl on the face plate it may be easier to work from the back (b).

THE SCREW POINT CHUCK

With the Black & Decker lathe you get an Internal Turning Attachment otherwise known as a screw point chuck. This is a special type of face plate chuck which holds small articles by a single woodscrew projecting from the centre. The setscrew that fastens the faceplate to the drill spindle can be unscrewed from the back of the faceplate with a spanner to let you get at the head of the woodscrew.

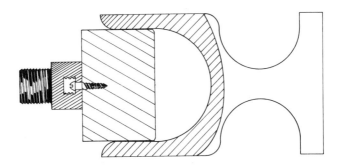

A useful way of turning articles with a hole or recess. The holder (here shown fixed on the screw point chuck) is turned from a piece of scrap wood.

To use the attachment for turning:

1 Mark the centre of your wood blank and drill a pilot hole for a No. 8 woodscrew.

2 Remove the setscrew from the back of the faceplate, and hold the wood blank against the front of the faceplate so that the pilot hole is in the centre.

3 Insert the chuck screw through the hole in the faceplate and tighten it home into the wood blank.

4 Replace the setscrew, tighten it with a spanner and screw it into the drill spindle.

You can now go ahead and turn the wood blank in the normal way, if necessary working from the back of the lathe to deal with the inside of hollow sections. There is no need to remove the screw chuck to mount the next blank; simply drill a central pilot hole for the chuck screw, unscrew the finished article and screw the blank back into its place.

If you do not want the chuck screw hole to appear in the finished article you can fix a piece of scrap wood to the attachment by the chuck screw to make a false faceplate and glue the blank to it, sandwiching a sheet of thin cardboard between the two faces. At the end of the job it is a simple matter to slice through the cardboard and sand the remains off the bottom of the finished article.

Where your blanks are all of the same outside diameter you can turn a recess in the false faceplate just big enough to be a tight, knock-in fit over the blank. Or if the blanks have a standard-sized hole, you can turn a spigot on the false faceplate to be a tight friction fit in the hole. You can extend this principle to let you turn all the faces of an article without showing screw marks or to provide

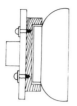 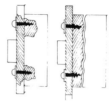

A false face plate turned from scrap wood will hold the workpiece without leaving screw holes. Left: Base of workpiece is a tight fit in recess in false face-plate. Right: Workpiece is glued to layer of paper stuck to false faceplate and is prised off after turning.

chucks for fast repetition work. In this case it would pay to have two or three attachments so that you could have separate friction chucks for each operation.

FINISHING

The smoothest finish you can produce with a tool can usually be improved still further by rubbing down with fine glass paper while the lathe is still running. Make a pad of soft cloth to use as a backing and hold the glasspaper against the front of the work and below the centre line so that your fingers are pointing the way the job is turning. Keep the glasspaper moving, do not press on hard, and do not dwell on any edges that you want to stay sharp. And, of course, have the tool rest right out of the way, or better still, remove it altogether.

HINTS ON THE LATHE ATTACHMENT

The lathe headstock is simply the Black & Decker horizontal drill stand mounted on the lathe bed, so you can turn it round and use it for any of the jobs you would do normally with the horizontal stand, using the flexible and rigid sanding discs (p 82), wire brushes, polishing buffs and so on. It will also take the disc sanding table attachment. The faceplate is identical with the rigid sanding disc and can be used for sharpening your lathe tools as described on p 105.

For further information connected with the Lathe Attachment see Grinding and Sharpening Tools (p 126).

It is only possible in this book to give you the basic information on using a lathe attachment. If you want to go further with this fascinating pastime you should either find an instructor or read a book dealing specifically with wood turning, such as *The Practical Wood Turner* by F. Pain (Woodworker Handbooks, Evans Brothers Limited, London). Many local education authorities organise courses in wood turning as part of their Adult Education programmes.

121

BENCH GRINDERS

A bench grinder is a useful power tool in any workshop, but if your interests include a lot of metal or woodwork it is not merely useful, but essential. For occasional small jobs like sharpening scissors or putting a new edge on a plane iron or wood working chisels, you can manage with a carborundum stone, an oilstone and a lot of patient manual grinding. A Black & Decker Disc Sander (p 88) makes an economical power grinder that will do all the average home handyman is likely to want. But for accurate grinding and for shaping tough or hardened steel quickly there is no substitute for the real tool.

Bench grinders all follow a standardised pattern. Two grinding wheels, one coarse and one fine, are mounted at opposite ends of the same shaft with the motor that drives them in between. The wheels are equipped with adjustable rests for the tools or whatever you are grinding, and enclosed in metal guards to protect you from flying particles of ground-off metal or dust formed by the wearing down of the wheels.

THE BLACK & DECKER D 370 POWER GRINDER

On the Black & Decker D 370 power grinder, two grinding wheels, 5 in. diameter and 1/2 in. wide are driven at a speed of 4,000 r.p.m. by a high speed motor through a helical reduction gear. The motor and gearbox are housed in a light alloy case between the wheels. Each wheel has an independent rest, the angle of which can be adjusted in relation to the wheel and moved in to compensate for the decreasing diameter of the wheel caused by wear.

Two steps of coarse adjustment are obtainable by reversing the rest of the fixing screw while fine adjustment is provided by a slot in the clamping plate. Robust metal guards around each wheel are open at the side to allow you to use the side of the wheel when you want to grind an absolutely flat face on a tool.

The grinder is fixed by four clamps which fit into slots in the base

The Black & Decker D370 power grinder is a sound investment for the serious do-it-yourself enthusiast and handyman. Sharpens tools of all kinds and shapes and smooths off any metal too hard for filing.

of the housing and are screwed down to the top of the bench. (If the top of your bench is made of metal or thin wood it may amplify the mechanical hum of the grinder. You can dampen the sound by mounting the grinder on a thick slab of wood and screwing that to the bench or by inserting a layer of sponge rubber between the base of the case and the bench. You should also fit rubber washers backed by steel washers at both ends of the fixing bolts (or under the heads of the screws if you are using wood screws for holding down the grinder). Your object should be to avoid direct metal-to-metal contact between the base of the grinder and the support.

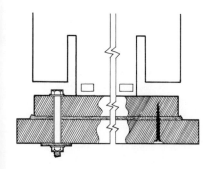

To cut down the noise made when the grinder is screwed on the bench, mount on a wooden base fastened down to the bench by bolts (left) or screws (right) insulated by felt or rubber foam between all bearing surfaces.

DON'T FORGET to keep a pair of industrial goggles or an eyeshield with your grinder and wear it during all grinding operations.

HOW TO USE THE BENCH GRINDER

Note: It is advisable to wear protective goggles for all work with either bench grinders or abrasive discs. Have them large enough to fit over your glasses if you wear them since flying particles of grit can pit optical glass.

First make sure that the grinder is securely fastened to the top of the work bench and that the three-core lead is connected to the mains by a 3-pin plug to a correctly earthed socket, preferably one fitted with a switch. (There is no switch on the grinder since this can be a source of danger on this class of power tool.)

Adjust both tool rests so that they are just clear of the wheels and tighten the fixing screws. For most grinding work you should have the rests horizontal; the angle adjustment is used mainly for grinding and sharpening cutting tools. Never have the rest so far away from the wheel that the metal you are grinding can wedge itself between the rest and the wheel. If this happens the results can be disastrous to both the grinder and the operator.

Apart from more accurate grinding and sharpening jobs, the bench grinder is useful for smoothing and trimming metal that you would normally do with a file or cold chisel, and for sharpening hardened steel that you cannot file. It is as well to practise with a few jobs of this kind for a start before you try anything you are likely to spoil.

So switch on the motor and give it a second or two to get up to speed. Now take the metal you want to grind, hold it flat on the rest and feed it towards the wheel until a stream of sparks shows that you have started grinding. The important thing from now on is to keep the work moving across the face of the wheel; do not keep it pressing against the same part all the time. Above all, do not force the job against the square corner of the wheel or you will quickly wear it away and the wheel will finish up with a rounded face.

Do not forget that a grinding wheel works by wearing away and exposing fresh, sharp-edged particles of grit. If it did not, the grit would soon lose its cutting edges and get clogged with dust to the point where it would stop cutting altogether. So whatever you are grinding, move it about the wheel to distribute the wear evenly and maintain a flat, square-cornered face.

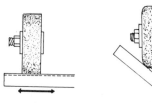

The right way: Keep the work moving from side to side across the face of the wheel. Right: Using the corner of the wheel is a quick way of removing metal— and spoiling the face for accurate grinding.

Do not use the grinder for grinding soft metals such as aluminium, brass, copper or lead or for plastics or in fact any materials that would clog the surface of the wheel. Once the cutting surface gets clogged and glazed the wheel will be useless until you can remove the choked layer of grit and expose a fresh cutting surface. You can try skimming the surface with the corner of the toothed edge of a broken hacksaw blade, but if that does not work either send it back to your Black & Decker Service Centre for attention, or take your grinder along to a local garage or factory where they have a diamond wheel dresser and ask them to skim the wheel. It is better to leave the wheel on the grinder—if you remove it for dressing it may not run true when you replace it on its original shaft.

Normally you should not grind anything on the side of the wheel because any wear there makes the face of the wheel narrower when you eventually grind down to it. In addition, there are times when you need an absolutely flat grinding surface, e.g. for the edges of many kinds of wood and metal cutting tools. For jobs like this it is useful to preserve the flat side of the wheel. Obviously before you break the rule and use the side of the wheel you should get as flat a face as possible on the tool by grinding it on the front of the wheel first, and only using the side for a final light application to get rid of the curvature left by the front of the wheel.

Your practice runs will teach you the art of grinding by using light pressure and keeping the job moving. They will also show you how quickly the edge you are grinding heats up. On industrial grinders the heat is carried away by a stream of water or cutting liquid, but the Black & Decker grinder is designed to be run dry and this means that you have to learn to avoid overheating.

If you are just using the wheel as a quick way of removing metal, overheating may not be important (although it does not do the wheel any good). But if you are grinding hardened and tempered cutting tools and let the cutting edge overheat, you will soften it and it will be useless until it has been re-hardened. This is a job for an expert, so learn to spot the danger signals so that you can stop grinding or move the wheel to another part of the work in time to avoid overheating. If you see the edge you are grinding glow red, or if it is bright steel and you see it turn dark blue, you have gone too far. You can keep a tin of cold water handy to cool the tool so long as you use it before the metal gets really hot—in fact as soon as you cannot bear to hold it against your hand. It is no use plunging the tool into cold water once you have let it overheat.

GRINDING AND SHARPENING TOOLS

After reading through the previous chapter you should know how to use your grinder for smoothing up rough metal edges and similar jobs. You will now be able to use your skill with the tool for more accurate grinding. This is where a Black & Decker bench grinder really pays off because you can use it for keeping a sharp edge on knives, scissors, wood and metal working tools and garden tools. You will save the cost and delay of having them ground, and they will always be sharp and ready to do a good job. When you cannot sharpen them yourself you are likely to go on putting off having the job done properly and spend most of your time working with blunt tools.

Grinding shapes the edge of the tool but you need an oilstone to add the finishing touch and for restoring its keenness from time to time.

WOODWORKING TOOLS
Woodworking hand tools are mostly ground on one side only; the other side is left flat. You grind the tool by resting the blade flat against the front of the rest and sloping upwards so that the ground edge rests on the face of the wheel. The grinding angle is important and it helps if you mark it on a cardboard protractor or cut a template to the correct angle and hold it on the top of the rest as a guide. Slide the blade from side to side so that it grinds evenly, and avoid overheating.

Once you have ground the bevel straight and square on to the blade you finish off the job on the oilstone. To do this, lay the stone on a flat surface so that it cannot rock or slide about and put a drop or two of light machine oil on the surface. Now hold the blade so that the bevel lies flat on the stone and then increase the angle by 5°

to $10°$ so that just the tip of the ground edge is in contact with the stone. Keep a steady pressure on the front of the blade with your fingers and rub the edge to and fro over the surface of the stone following a narrow oval path. Keep the angle of the blade constant while you do this and from time to time wipe the oil off the edge and inspect it. When you see a bright strip of metal stretching from one side to the other, give the blade a final wipe and then feel the edge on the flat side. You will notice a slight raised burr. This has to be removed before the job is finished. You can either draw the edge backwards and forwards over the top of the bench at a steep angle until the burr breaks away or you can lay the blade flat on the oilstone and remove the burr with a few gentle rubs. This process of finishing on the oilstone is known as honing.

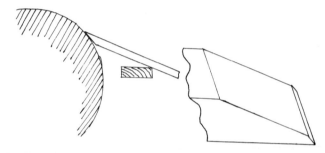

You sharpen a carpenter's chisel by first grinding one side on the wheel (left) and then honing a second bevel edge at a slightly steeper angle on an oil stone (right).

This is the way you sharpen chisels, plane irons and similar wood-cutting tools. The same method is used for gouges but with these tools you have to roll the blade from side to side as you grind and hone the cutting edge. If you do not feel skillful enough to do the final work on the oilstone you can buy an adjustable holder or jig that makes the job easy. The grinding and honing angles for the common woodworking tools are given in the table below.

Tool	Grinding Angle	Honing Angle
Chisel (paring)	$20°-25°$	$30°$
Chisel (chopping)	$30°$	$35°$
Plane (trying and smoothing)	$25°$	$30°$
Plane (block)	$30°$	$35°$

When tools of this type lose their edge, a rub on the oilstone is all they need to make them keen again. However, after a time the edge creeps back and takes too long to stone sharp. When they reach that state you will have to grind a new face and start again.

WOOD TURNING TOOLS

These require different treatment. The chisels are ground on each face; the two bevels are identical and include an angle of 45° (this is the angle usually recommended but it is not critical to a degree or two either way). Gouges are ground on the outside face only. The angle should be at least 45° for working inside bowls although for outside turning it can be a few degrees less.

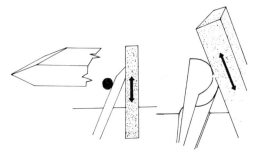

A wood turning chisel is ground on both faces (left). This tool is honed by holding it against a stop and moving the oil stone across the whole of the ground face (centre). A gouge is honed in the same way (right). Wood turning tools have no second bevel.

The major difference between these and hand tools is that the turning tools have no second bevel. In turning, while the edge is cutting, the bevel rubs on the work and prevents the tool from digging in, but the narrow bevel produced by honing would not let this happen. So after you have ground the wood turning tool to the correct angle and you come to hone the edge, the whole width of the bevel must rub on the oilstone, not just the tip.

Honing a wood turning tool this way is easier if you hold the tool still and move the oilstone. You rest the stone on a flat surface, usually the bench top, and slide it backwards and forwards while you press the bevel of the tool against the vertical side of the stone, supporting the blade of the tool either in a notch cut in the edge of the bench or against any kind of stop you care to improvise. This way you can maintain the tool at a fixed angle and actually see the contact between the bevel and the stone, making it easier to keep the bevel flat against the stone.

Honing a chisel this way is fairly easy; a gouge is more difficult because you have to turn it as you hone. This is one of the jobs you have to learn by practising but it is worth the trouble because you need sharp tools for wood turning, and you cannot remove the burr from the inside curve of the gouge with a flat oilstone. For this you need a small rounded oilstone that you can buy at your tool counter. Ask for a gouge slip.

SCRAPING TOOLS

These tools for your wood turning lathe are flat on the top face (which never needs regrinding) and the scraping edge is ground at an angle of 70° to 80° – chiefly to provide some clearance between the wood and the tool below the edge. To grind a scraping tool you simply set the tool rest at about 10° to 20° to the horizontal and grind the edge of the scraper with the tool lying flat on the rest. You can make very effective scraping tools from old flat files. Simply grind away the teeth from the top surface and then grind the cutting edge of the tool to the shape you want—rounded, square or skew— with the file flat on the rest. (Although it is not necessary to grind the teeth off the underside of the tool, you should grind away the sharp tops of the teeth so that you can manipulate the tool on the tool rest of the grinder and the lathe.)

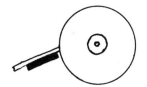

Grinding a scraping tool for wood turning. The rest should be set at an angle of 10°-20° to the horizontal.

WOOD CARVING TOOLS

There is a bevel on both sides of the edge of these tools. You can grind and hone the outside bevel exactly like a wood turning gouge, but for the smaller inside bevel you need a shaped oilstone slip, rounded for the normal gouge and triangular for the V-tool.

CARPENTERS' DRILL BITS

It is usually easier to grind these by hand with a carborundum slip but many types can be ground quicker on the bench grinder. The ground face is easy to recognise and so long as it is open-ended you can grind it on the wheel. Some bits have the cutting edge in between the centre screw and a spur on the outside. These can only be ground with a specially narrow wheel or with a carborundum slip.

TWIST DRILLS

These can be sharpened on the bench grinder but you need a lot of experience to do the job properly. For most ordinary handymen the best thing to do is to keep the drill sharp as long as possible and then either take a collection of worn drills to a tool shop for resharpening or replace them with new drills. Modern high speed steel drills will last a very long time with the kind of occasional use they get in the amateur's workshop. You can extend the life of a drill by only using it on the materials and at the speeds it is designed for. Do not let it overheat. Keep it cutting: do not let it just rub. Keep it lubricated when drilling metal and when you are drilling a deep hole, withdraw the drill frequently so that the flutes will not get clogged and make the drill overheat. This is just as important when you are drilling hard wood like oak as it is when you are drilling metal.

If you particularly want to sharpen your own twist drills you can buy a special grinding jig with complete instructions that make the job easy. But you can probably buy all the new drills you are likely to need for very much less than the cost of the jig.

MASONRY DRILLS

The tungsten carbide drill tips are too hard to be ground on an ordinary wheel. These drills have to be sharpened on a diamond grit wheel but most tool dealers offer an exchange service and will either sharpen a drill for you or give you a resharpened drill in exchange for your old one at a fraction of the cost of a new drill. Or you can usually return the drill to the manufacturer by post and have it resharpened for a standard charge stated on the card or leaflet that you get with the drill.

KNIVES

Knives have a wedge-shaped blade which is so thin that the natural angle of the edge would be too fine to stand up to hard work. The extreme edge must be ground to a more obtuse angle by bevelling each side. You can do this in one continuous stroke along each side of the blade, or you can produce it by rubbing the blade on an oil-stone. You should aim at producing a cutting edge with an angle of $20°$. After several resharpenings the cutting edge will wear back to the thicker part of the blade and when that happens you thin the blade down by grinding the whole surface. This is one of the jobs that you can safely do on the side of the stone because it will wear it evenly and not leave scores or hollows.

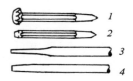

Scissors or shears can be sharpened on the grinding wheel without separating the blades-so long as the corner of the stone is undamaged.

Top: Sharpening a cold chisel: (1) before, (2) after. Bottom: A screwdriver blade should be hollow ground (3) A rounded tip (4) is apt to slip.

SCISSORS

Slight wear can be corrected by sharpening on the bench grinder. For this there is no need to take the blades apart. Open the blades as wide as they will go, lay one blade flat on the rest parallel with the front face of the fine grinding stone and check that you can get the edge of the stone right up to the root of the blade. Now set the angle of the rest at $10°$ to grind the blade of the scissors, so that the cutting edge will have an angle of $80°$. (For heavy duty, this angle can be as much as $90°$.)

Now draw each blade in turn lightly across the face of the stone in a single movement. Repeat this just enough to restore the sharp edge. Then, if necessary, rub the inside face of the blade with an oilstone to remove the grinding burr.

Do not attempt to grind the inside faces of the blade; these are usually hollow-ground on a machine and the accurate curve would be ruined by hand grinding.

SHEARS, HEDGE CLIPPERS AND SIMILAR TOOLS

These are ground in the same way as scissors and the same precautions about grinding the inside faces apply.

When you are grinding a long continuous edge like that on knives, scissors and shears, ease the pressure as you approach the tip or it will overheat and destroy the temper of the steel. This is because at the pointed tip there is not enough metal to draw the heat away and stop the temperature rising dangerously.

SCREWDRIVERS

Screwdrivers are ground by steadying the shank against the edge of the rest with the tip of the blade pointing upwards and lying flat on the stone. Adjust the angle of the blade with the wheel at rest so that the curve of the wheel will hollow the blade slightly, making it fractionally thinner behind the edge. A blade ground this way tends not to slip out of the slot in the head of the screw.

COLD CHISELS

These are for cutting metal and can be ground and sharpened by applying them to the wheel pointing upwards with the shank steadied against the tool rest as in grinding screwdrivers. In this case you grind to form a strong edge with an angle of around $40°$ for the softer metals like brass and copper to $70°$ for tough steel, so $55°-60°$ should serve you for general workshop use.

After some use the top of a cold chisel spreads out and cracks around the edges. When this happens small chips are apt to fly off and cause accidents, so from time to time grind the top of the chisel with a slight inward taper.

CENTRE PUNCHES

Grind these tools by holding them at an angle to the wheel and slowly turning the shank in your fingers. A punch used simply for marking the circumference of a hole (p 34) should be ground to a $60°$ point whereas one intended to give a start to the drill point should be ground to $90°$.

When the wheels on your Black & Decker bench grinder have worn down so far that you can no longer adjust the tool rest close to the face, they should be renewed. You change wheels by unscrewing the spindle nut, removing the worn wheel and chucking plate and then fit the new wheel, replacing everything in the reverse order. Remember that the right-hand spindle has a right-handed thread and the left-hand spindle a left-handed thread. Always make sure that the new wheel is marked as suitable for use at 4,000 r.p.m. or more.

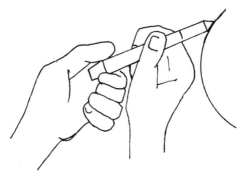

Sharpen a centre punch by twisting the shank in your fingers as you grind. Keep the end of the punch moving from side to side and you won't leave a groove in the wheel.

EXTRAS TO HELP YOU

Your power tool is a regular Jack-of-all-trades and its usefulness goes beyond the applications described so far. Once you have covered all the basic uses you will find yourself thinking up other ways for using your drill as a power unit to make things easy. We know of one enthusiast whose wife likes to preserve the produce of their small apple orchard by bottling the fruit. He speeds the operation by turning his variable speed Black & Decker drill into an apple peeler. To do this he mounts the drill in the horizontal drill stand and pushes the apple on to a spade-ended spike gripped in the chuck. Then, with the drill set to turn at about 100 r.p.m. he slices off the skin in a continuous paring with a kitchen peeler just as though he were turning a piece of wood on the face plate of the lathe attachment. Once you master the knack you can change apples without stopping the drill.

This is just one of the many ideas that power tool users come up with. If you have any ideas like this remember that a power tool has its limitations and that it is not designed to drive a home-made concrete mixer or a gem-stone polisher that you want to run non-stop for several weeks.

There is an ever increasing number of accessories made by power tool manufacturers, including Black & Decker, for doing a wider and wider range of jobs from cake mixing to paint spraying. Some of the gadgets will be worth adding to your tool kit, some will not; it all depends on how often you want to do the particular job for which the accessory is designed, but if you get enjoyment out of playing with your power tool and a particular gadget offers you more fun, why not go ahead and spoil yourself even if you cannot justify the purchase on any other grounds? The sort of relaxation you can enjoy from just playing around with a new gadget is exactly what some people are trying to get when they pay for expensive nature cures or indoor exercising machines or therapeutic treatment.

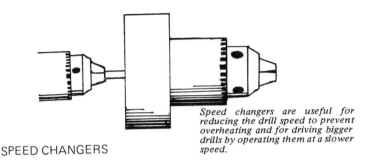

Speed changers are useful for reducing the drill speed to prevent overheating and for driving bigger drills by operating them at a slower speed.

SPEED CHANGERS

A number of accessories should be included in the list of what-to-buy-next that most handymen keep, if only in their minds. One of these, the drill speed changing attachment, should top your list if your power tool is a single speed model. There are several proprietary makes, all following the same general principle with a spindle at one end that you grip in the chuck of your power tool and a chuck at the other that turns at 1/4 to 1/2 of the speed. And the chuck at the business end usually takes a larger size drill because its slower speed gives it a proportionately more powerful turning force. So as well as stepping down the speed of your drill—which is useful for preventing over-heating when you are drilling masonry or very tough steel—it enables you to use a bigger diameter drill.

You have to remember that the cost of a speed changer which will fit any drill has to include the cost of an independent chuck, usually larger and more expensive than the one in your drill already.

RIGHT ANGLE DRILLING ATTACHMENTS

The overall length of a simple power tool is something like 8 in. and the drill bit can extend this up to 12 in. There are times when you would like to drill a hole in a position where there is not that much space available, and several manufacturers make right angle drilling attachments with which you can drill in confined spaces like this. The attachment usually consists of a set of right-angle bevel gears in a gearcase with a spindle to grip in the chuck of your power tool and a chuck pointing at right angles to take the drill bit for boring the hole.

Even where there is room for the normal power tool to operate there may not be enough for you to get behind it and apply the pressure, e.g. when you are working in a narrow cupboard. The right angle attachment enables you to get in line with the actual drill while you hold the power tool to one side or the other.

THE BLACK & DECKER RIGHT ANGLE SPEED CHANGER

By incorporating a speed change in the right angle drilling attachment Black & Decker have combined the functions of both the above accessories in a single unit. There are two other advantages. First, the gearbox fits on any Black & Decker power drill in place of the existing chuck while the chuck itself fits on to the right angle spindle. This means that you save the cost of the extra chuck. Then you can fit the changer so that the speed change works either way, giving a reduction to 1/2 the normal speed of the power drill or an increase of X 2: e.g. with a Black & Decker Super D 500 drill you have a choice of no-load speeds of 2,900 r.p.m. without the changer, 1,450 r.p.m. using the changer one way round or 5,800 r.p.m. the other way round. In practice with a reasonable load on the drill the speeds would be more like 2,500, 1,250 and 5,000.

The lower speed obtainable with the changer is useful for drilling masonry, tiles, extra large holes in metal and wood and for driving a polisher. At the higher speed you can drill holes up to 1/8 in. diameter with less risk of breakage and you will also make a better job of disc sanding.

The right angle drive solves the problem of drilling in confined spaces, such as through floor joints, and is ideal for polishing because the closer support gives you much steadier control over the movement of the polishing head.

The Black & Decker right angle speed changer can be fitted to other makes of pistol-grip drill by fitting a chuck adaptor at one end of the drive and a suitable Black & Decker chuck to the other. In this case the power drill chuck is left in position to grip the chuck adaptor spindle but its presence does not affect the overall length of the business end.

When you are working with the right angle drill attachment you grasp it firmly and guide the drill with the hand holding the attachment, not the one supporting the actual drill.

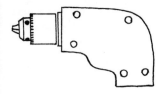

The Black & Decker right angle speed changer attachment fits in place of the chuck for drilling holes in confined spaces. The chuck ends are interchangeable giving a choice of faster or slower speeds.

CAR POLISHERS

If you take pride in the appearance of your car you can make the job of polishing a lot easier by getting your power tool on to the job. All you need is the normal rubber backing pad used for flexible disc sanding and a polishing bonnet. The bonnet is simply a lambswool cover that you fit over the face of the backing pad and hold in place by tightening and tying off a drawstring at the back of the pad. You tuck the ends of the drawstring out of the way and you are ready to start polishing. You can fit this type of polishing bonnet to any make of power tool if you use a flexible back mounted on a spindle that you grip in the chuck. However, the chuck and spindle add extra inches to the overall length of the tool and make it difficult to control. It is much easier to get a smooth sweep and an even polish when the backing pad fits right up against the business end of the power tool in place of the chuck.

A lambswool polishing bonnet fastened over a flexible back sanding disc makes a high speed polisher for cars or furniture. The polisher replaces the chuck in any Black & Decker home user power tool.

BLACK & DECKER CAR POLISHING EQUIPMENT

There is an integral Black & Decker car polisher which is marketed for the benefit of car owners who want to keep one tool specially for this job and who probably have an independent power drill that they want to keep that way. This tool is simply the body of a power drill with a flexible backing pad for the polishing bonnet screwed directly in to the end of the drive spindle where the chuck normally goes. It makes a compact unit that is easy to hold firmly without dithering as you sweep it over the waxed surface. If you already own one of the Black & Decker home user drills you can turn it into a car polisher by simply unscrewing the chuck and replacing it with the screw-in flexible pad and polishing bonnet.

An alternative polishing arrangement is to add a Black & Decker right angle speed changer with the polisher fitted to the slow speed end. This has the advantage of giving you firmer control of the revolving bonnet and allowing you to use more pressure on the surface without overloading the motor. (For the same reason, if your drill is a 2-speed model you should engage the low gear for polishing.)

You can also fit the bonnet over a chuck-held backing pad but this js difficult to manage because your supporting hand is too far away from the revolving bonnet to hold it steady.

POWER POLISHING

To give your car body the complete treatment you should first prepare the surface for applying the wax polish. Fairly new car bodies will only need a thorough wash with warm detergent or one of the many proprietary car shampoos. Older cars may need a more drastic treatment with a mild abrasive type of cleaner to remove the grubby, discoloured top layer of paint. In either case, you should wash over the body with clean warm water to get rid of the cleaner.

Apply the wax polish in long straight overlapping sweeps when the surface is absolutely dry. Do not try to do the whole body in one attempt. Tackle it in small manageable sections, starting with the roof and then working around the sides. Plan the operation in such a way that you can polish each section without trailing the cable over a part that you have already either waxed or polished.

You use the polisher with broad straight sweeping strokes, covering the particular area in a ziz-zag pattern tilting the power unit so that only half of the face of the bonnet is in contact with the surface. Press lightly and ease off the pressure even more if you hear the motor slowing down.

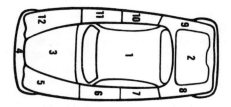

When using the polisher on your car, tackle the job methodically in sections so that the mains cable does not trail over the parts you have polished.

As you work the bonnet will tend to get loaded with dirt. When this happens run it against the sharp inside edge of the bumper for a second or two. This should get rid of the dirt and you can continue polishing. But from time to time, depending on how often you polish the car, the bonnet will get too soiled to respond to this treatment and you will have to wash it. Moisten the front of the pad with warm water, then work washing powder into the fibres with your fingers, and finally rinse clean, keeping the back of the bonnet as dry as you can. You can then spin the bonnet on the drill to get rid of the surplus water and dry it off in a warm place. To keep it from picking up dust and grit that would cause scratches, store the bonnet in a polythene bag.

FURTHER USE FOR THE CAR POLISHER

As the car polisher is basically the drill power unit fitted with a polishing head instead of a chuck, you can use it to power any of the Black & Decker attachments or mount it in a horizontal or vertical stand for flexible and rigid disc sanding, wire brushing, grinding and so on. You can also turn it into a drill by fitting a drill chuck in place of the flexible backing pad and you can use it to power the lathe attachment.

THE BLACK & DECKER SCREWDRIVER ATTACHMENT

This tool is not for everybody but if you are making or assembling a steady flow of articles involving a lot of woodscrewing then it might save you time and effort far beyond its initial cost.

The attachment provides a quick way of driving wood screws inserted in prepared holes in the woodwork. It incorporates a finder which automatically locates the screwdriver bit in the slot and an automatic clutch which slips once the screw has been driven home. While it is designed to screw in place of the chuck of any of the Black & Decker range of home user drills, it can be adapted for use in the chuck of any other make of portable power tool.

The attachment is supplied in two principal units, the bit and finder assembly and the body which incorporates the clutch. With the body you get two alternative adaptors. One is for screwing directly into the drive spindle of the power tool in place of the chuck. The other adaptor has a plain drive spindle with three flats to hold in the chuck of any power drill. The bit and finder are held in position by a ball catch inside the body of the attachment. You can remove it to change over to a different size screwdriver bit by giving it a sharp tug. The bit and finder supplied with the attachment are suitable for screw sizes from No. 5 to No. 9 but you can buy an alternative fitting to take screw sizes from No. 8 to No. 12.

The size and length of screw you can drive depends mainly on the speed of the drill as shown in the table below:

Screw Size	Pilot Drill Size		Clearance Drill Size		Length Up To	Recommended Drill Speed
No.	Drill No.	Fraction (in.)	Drill No. or Letter	Fraction (in.)	(in.)	(r.p.m.)
6	35	7/64	25	5/32	2	1,750–3,000
8	29	1/8	15	3/16	2 1/2	1,000–1,750
10	22	5/32	3	7/32	2 1/2	1,000–1,750
12	14	11/64	C	1/4	2 1/2	600–1,000

In fact even for the smallest sizes the screwdriver works best at speeds no higher than 2,000 r.p.m. If you have a single speed power tool that runs faster than this you will get better results by using a speed changing attachment, e.g. the Black & Decker right angle speed changer or one of the proprietary makes of straight through speed changer.

The Black & Decker screwdriver attachment is a time saver when you have a lot of screws to drive. It incorporates a finder to guide the screwdriver into the slot and a clutch which slips when the screw is tight.

WIRE BRUSHES

Take a circular brush made of hard steel wires and spin it around with a power drill and you have a wonderful tool for getting rust and corrosion off metal surfaces that you want to paint. A power driven wire brush is also ideal for decarbonising cylinder heads, exhaust manifolds and silencers or for cleaning out flues in central heating boilers and almost every job that you used to do with the old hand-powered wire brush. Of course, the power brush does the job in a tenth of the time and makes no demands on your muscles. So if your do-it-yourself activities include painting metal work in or out of doors, car maintenance or any other jobs involving rust and corrosion, you will find it worthwhile to invest in at least one wire brush for a start, although you will probably end up with a collection.

You can buy all kinds of wire brush for your power tool. Some have the brush mounted on a short spindle that you grip in the chuck of your power drill; some fit on an arbor held in the chuck and can be interchanged without disturbing the chuck, and another type, e.g. the Black & Decker wire cup brush, screws into the drive spindle in place of the chuck.

Wire wheel brushes have the wires mounted radially and are held on an arbor gripped in the drill chuck. This type does the brushing with the outside edge and works best if the drill is mounted on a fixed bench stand, e.g. the Black & Decker horizontal drill stand, as this leaves you with both hands free to manipulate the metal you are wire brushing. It is not easy to hold the power tool steady in your hands while you use the edge of a brush of this type. So it is more suitable for work that you can bring to the bench than for using for de-rusting iron rain guttering in situ, and similar jobs.

The cup type of wire brush, as the name indicates, has the wires arranged in a hollow circle with the business ends pointing forward. You use it in much the same way as you use a flexible disc-sander, pressing only one side of the brush against the surface and keeping it moving all the time in wide sweeps. This type of wire brush is easier to control with the drill held in your hand and it is the one to choose for use in a portable tool.

You can buy sets of wire brushes in a range of shapes and sizes for specialised jobs like decarbonising engines.

THE BLACK & DECKER WIRE BRUSHES
Black & Decker make both a 4 in. diameter wire wheel brush and a 3 in. diameter cup brush. As explained above, the wheel brush which you mount on a chuck-held arbor is more suitable for use as a bench tool with the drill mounted in the horizontal bench stand.

The cup brush can be used either as a bench mounted or portable tool. It screws into the power drill drive spindle in place of the chuck and so makes a more compact and easily handled assembly than you get with a wire brush held in the drill chuck.

Both brushes should be run at 2–3000 r.p.m. The cup brush should be tilted so that only part of the edge bears on the work and you should hold it so that the movement of the brush tends to force

140

Many kinds of rotary cutter fit in the power tool chuck for rasping or routing jobs.

Two Black & Decker wire brushes: the cup type and the wheel type.

the wires inwards instead of splaying them out.

After a time the sharp cutting edges of the wires will become dull. When this happens you can sharpen them again by simply holding the brush in your hand and turning it against a revolving grindstone.

Warning: When sanding or wire brushing you should always wear protective goggles and in any case make a habit of working with your face out of the line of fire of any grit or metal dust flung off by the revolving tool.

ROTARY CUTTING TOOLS

You can now buy a wide variety of rotary cutting tools including files, rasps, routers and variously shaped profiling cutters which are designed to be gripped in the chuck of a power drill.

The rotary rasp type of tool is principally for roughing out and shaping wood, laminates and plastics. These tools are made in a number of different shapes, or you can buy them in sets which usually give you a choice of spherical, conical and cylindrical heads formed on the standard 1/4 in. shank to fit into the drill chuck.

You can work freehand with these tools, holding the power drill in your hands, but it is difficult to control the action this way and the cutter is apt to chatter and leave ridges or slip and score the surface alongside. You get the best results by mounting the power drill in a vertical or horizontal drill stand which leaves both your hands free to manipulate the work.

Profiling sheet or board is easier if you have the drill in a vertical stand and rest the work flat on the base. You can adjust the height of the drill carriage so that the tool engages the edge of the work at the correct depth, or lay a piece of board on the drill stand base to raise the work so that the cutter can cover the full depth right down to the under surface. With this set-up you can draw the shape you want to produce on the surface of the work and then slide it around in contact with the cutter to clear away the waste material right up to the line.

Cutting tools of this type do not leave a really smooth finish unless they rotate at a really high speed (around 20,000 r.p.m.) and are fitted with a motor of at least 1 h.p. The sort you use in a home user power drill is apt to leave a rough finish, but you can always complete the job with a sanding tool such as the drum type described above.

Rasps and other woodworking tools should be run at the fastest speed if you are using a 2-speed drill. Rotary files used on metal require slow speed. If used in a single speed drill you should fit them in a speed reducing attachment or they will quickly lose their sharpness.

It is not possible to cover all the individual makers' products here, but you can get all the information you need from the advertisement pages of such handyman publications as *Do it yourself* Magazine.

FLEXIBLE DRIVE

You use a flexible drive when you want to do small drilling, grinding or polishing jobs which are not conveniently placed for working with the tool held in the drill chuck. These accessories are made by several manufacturers but they all work in the same way.

The drive consists of a flexible steel cable made either of stranded wire or a coiled spring, running inside an outer casing of braided or coiled steel wire. One end of the driving cable terminates in a short steel rod that you grip in the chuck of the power drill and the other end carries the miniature chuck that holds the tool.

To use the drive you must fix the power tool in a bench stand. This can be either vertical or horizontal, but a vertical stand is best as it prevents side wear on the drive cable bearing. You use the miniature chuck to hold a small drill or a tiny grinding wheel moulded on to a suitable spindle. These wheels are obtainable from tool stores in a variety of shapes—drums, cones, discs and so on. (You can improvise a polishing head by simply winding a strip of cloth soaked in metal polish around the wheel.)

The chuck end of the flexible drive casing is shaped to form a hand grip allowing you to manipulate the tool like a brush or a pencil. As the diameter of the tool is small you have to run it as fast as possible, i.e. on the high speed of a 2-speed drill.

This accessory is useful for such jobs as grinding and polishing the ports of a car or motorcycle engine, shaping and sharpening small tools and drilling small holes where it is easier to move the drill about than the workpiece or the power tool.

You can also use the grinding wheels for engraving designs on glass surfaces, flat or curved. If you want to do this you will have to provide a supply of lubricant such as paraffin or turpentine, by either dripping or brushing it on to the surface as you work.

THE BLACK & DECKER PAINT STIRRER

This accessory makes an easy job of mixing paint that has been standing for some time. Just fit it in your power tool chuck like a drill, immerse the stirrer in the paint and switch on. Be sure to switch off *before* you lift the stirrer out of the paint.

THE BLACK & DECKER WHEEL ARBOR

The wheel arbor spindle fits in the drill chuck and provides you with a power driven shaft on which you can mount a grinding wheel, polishing buff, wire wheel brush, and many other circular form tools and cutters. These are held between two washers and secured by a nut on the end of the shaft. The nut has a left hand thread; a right hand thread would be slackened off by the rotation of the spindle.

POWER TOOLS IN THE GARDEN: MOWING

You can please yourself about jobs in the home, but if you have even a small garden there are two jobs you cannot ignore. Unless you can afford to pay a gardener you have to mow lawns and trim hedges. For most people these have always been chores that use up spare time that they would rather spend in other ways. Dedicated gardeners would rather be in the flower border, vegetable garden or potting shed and the other sort would rather be in a deck chair. But right through the summer months these two jobs have to be done and you no sooner do them than they need to be done again.

However, the power tool revolution has changed the picture. Today you can buy electric power tools that make lawn mowing as easy as using a vacuum cleaner and hedge trimming a matter of minutes instead of hours. The principal tools that have made this possible are rotary electric mowers like the Black & Decker Lawnderette and electric hedge trimmers, both mains and battery operated, like those in the Black & Decker range.

Most people are familiar with the cylinder type of lawn mower where you have a construction like a circular cage of strips of steel with sharp edges spinning around and cutting the grass against a stationary blade. The spinning cutter flips the chopped off bits of grass into a grass box which you lift off and empty when it gets full, usually every two or three minutes.

Cylinder type lawn mowers use a set of revolving blades assembled like a cylindrical cage around a power driven shaft. The edges of the blades cut the grass against a fixed knife under the mower. If the grass is long or wet it tends to lie flat and let the blades pass over without cutting it. Loose stones can easily damage or break the blades.

This sort of mower is always hard to push around the lawn. And making it wider so that it will cut more grass and get the job done more quickly makes it harder to push, so you are not much better off. Years ago manufacturers added a petrol engine driving unit but it is still heavy and awkward to handle, often infuriatingly difficult to start and always liable to be put out of action by a stone in the wrong place. The grass box and its load have become heavier and the box seems to need emptying twice as often. Usually it is noisy too because the easiest way to cheapen the cost of a petrol engine is to fit a smaller silencer. From time to time the blades need resharpening which can only be done with skilled labour and special machinery, both making it an expensive job.

This may sound unfair to a type of machine that has been in popular use for years. In fact these machines are quite useful for cutting large lawns where the work is mostly in straight stretches but on the smaller lawns where there are borders, garden sheds, sundials, lily ponds, bird baths and other garden ornaments, the traditional mower is a long way from being the ideal tool. And it cannot cut long wet grass because the roller in front of the cutter presses the grass down and the blades miss it.

The rotary mower is another type that has been in use for some time. With this type the grass is cut by a fan shaped rotor driven by a petrol engine. It cuts the grass mostly by the sheer speed of the blade hitting the grass. This type has the big advantage that it will cut long or wet grass. The sharpness of the blades is not very important and it is not serious if it hits a stone but the other disadvantages of weight, awkward handling in small spaces, and noise are still there.

Rotary mowers have the revolving blades mounted radially on the end of a vertical power driven shaft. There is no stationary knife and the blades cut principally by their high speed of rotation. Sharpness is not important and there is no difficulty in cutting long or wet grass. This type is not so easily damaged by loose stones and blades are cheap to replace.

Because of these problems manufacturers have never stopped looking at other ways of doing the job. However, from the point of view of the man with the modest garden, nothing really exciting happened until Black & Decker introduced the Lawnderette rotary electric lawn mower. There have been plenty of electric powered machines and a whole series of petrol driven rotary mowers, but the Lawnderette combines the special advantages of the rotary principle with smooth reliable electric power.

THE BLACK & DECKER LAWNDERETTE

The Black & Decker Lawnderette is a rotary type mower. The Economy model costs less than many unpowered lawn mowers. The machine is controlled by an on-off trigger switch with lock-on button on the handle.

This new machine is about as simple as a mower can get. The cutter is a strip of tempered steel fixed at the centre on the end of a Black & Decker electric power unit which spins it round 4,000 times a minute, slicing cleanly through the grass even when small stones and grit have dulled the edge. The motor is enclosed in a housing mounted on top of the steel cowl which covers the cutter and the whole assembly rides on a split roller at the back and two wheels at the front. You can adjust the cutting height by setting the front wheels in Low, Medium or High positions provided by shaped slots in the housing. The wheels are released to adjust the height by slacking off the spindle nuts. (On the earlier models the cutting height was adjusted by inserting spacing washers on the driving spindle behind the cutter.)

The moulded handle pistol grip is mounted on the end of a steel tube which connects it to the mower assembly. It houses the on-off switch trigger which has a locking button which can be pressed to keep the motor switched on and is released by a second pressure on the switch trigger.

OVERLOAD CUTOUT

The moulded handle also houses an automatic thermal switch which switches off the motor if it should be accidentally overloaded. You should, however, switch off the trigger switch as soon as the cutout operates. When you have found and cleared the cause of the overloading you press the cutout button to reset the cutout and restart the motor by pressing the switch trigger in the usual way.

DOUBLE INSULATION

The electric motor is of the double insulated type and needs no earth connexion. It is connected to the mains through the switch in the hand grip and a short length of 2-core cable terminating in a 2-pin connector. The socket end of the connector is fitted to the end of the mains lead. This may be either a 2- or 3-core cable, but only the live and neutral conductors are connected to the 2-pin connector. (See also p 164.)

ECONOMY MODEL

A new low-cost model, D 485 Lawnderette, is now available. This model, while lacking some of the refinements of the D 484, has a comparable performance and has been developed to serve the owners of small gardens who would normally have put up with the disadvantages of a cheap hand mower. For roughly the same price they now enjoy the ease and speed of electric mowing.

The rear roller on the more expensive models makes it possible to produce a striped effect by cutting alternate swathes in opposite directions. This is not possible with the low-cost D 485 model because this runs on wheels at the rear as well as the front.

HOW TO USE THE LAWNDERETTE

The Lawnderette weighs only 11 1/2 lb (the D 485 model at only 10 lb is even lighter) so handling is no problem whatever your age or sex. Once you have got your lawn into shape, keeping it trim with the Lawnderette is as easy as using a vacuum cleaner. The only parts of the job that call for care are handling the mains cable, cutting long grass and neglected lawns, and cutting around verges.

HANDLING THE MAINS CABLE.
This is something you will have to master from the start so this is the right place to discuss it.

First of all you will need to buy a length of suitable cable long enough to stretch comfortably from the nearest power point in the house, garage or workshop to the farthest point on the lawn you are going to cut. Make allowance for the diversions around flower beds and any other obstacles to the straight run of the cable. You can use 2-core cable as the Lawnderette is double insulated and does not need an earth wire. If the cable is of the right type, preferably Black & Decker standard 2-core extension cable, you can have up to 200 ft connecting the Lawnderette to the power point. For working at more than 200 ft the resistance of the cable will prevent the motor from developing its full power and you will have to make special arrangements (see Power Tool Electrics, p 164).

The ideal way of storing the cable is to wind it on to a portable drum like the Black & Decker cable reel (p 168). It is not an easy job to coil up to 100 ft of electric cable by hand without forming kinks and knots and wasting a lot of time unravelling it. It *can* be done by laying it on the ground in a figure 8 formation, as sailors do with lengths of rope, but a portable cable reel is the only satisfactory answer.

You cannot turn the cable reel once you have plugged the extension cable into the mains socket, so decide on the length you are going to need and snake it out along the side of the lawn, clear of the grass—a path is the obvious place. Once the cable is connected, you can go ahead and mow the lawn without any fear of snarling it up so long as you work to a regular pattern. If you are right handed, use your right hand to guide the mower and your left to handle the cable. Hold the cable so that there is about 3 ft of slack between your hand and the connector. Pull off the slack as you need it and when you want to make a right hand turn at the top of a strip, jerk a loop of cable beyond the turning point so that there will be enough slack to pass behind you when you change direction. Work across the lawn, away from the parked cable, mowing up and down, each time slightly overlapping the previous strip and always turning away from the cable between finishing one strip and starting back the other way. This way you never risk crossing over the cable and cutting it. When you have mown the far side of the lawn you can disconnect the cable and wind it back on to the reel. The lawn should now have the neat striped pattern that all gardeners like to see.

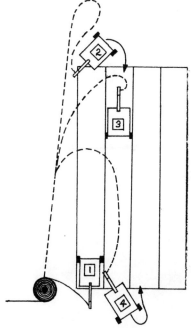

The mains lead to an electric mower can't get in your way so long as you work to a system. Lay out the cable along one side of the grass to be cut and work away from it in alternate to and fro passes until you reach the far side.

CUTTING LONG GRASS AND NEGLECTED LAWNS

With the Lawnderette you can cut long and wet grass but you will have to go to a little trouble to avoid overloading the motor. This happens if long stems wind around the cutter, become wedged against the cover and act like a brake. To avoid this, first set the cutter as high as it will go. Then lower the handle to tilt up the front end of the Lawnderette and advance it a little way into the long grass. Slowly raise the handle as you work the mower backwards and forwards until the front wheels are resting on the ground. Now lower the handle and take another bite at the next bit of long grass. From time to time, especially if you hear the motor slowing down, switch off the motor, disconnect the mains plug and clean out the inside of the cutter cover. Remove any long grass that may have wrapped itself around the cutter drive. You can make the job easier if you rake off the cut grass as you go so that the cutter blade does not pick it up again. (Once the grass is down to the normal length you will not need to do this.)

On the latest model, if you force the pace and overload the motor, the cutout will operate and switch it off before you can do any damage. When this happens, go through the cleaning drill and then switch on again, but this time let the motor run without cutting for a couple of minutes to give the built in fan a chance to cool it down.

If a lawn has been neglected for months or years it will be choked with dead grass and make hard going for the motor. You can make the job of rehabilitation a lot easier if you go over the lawn first with a grass rake and tease out all the old grass.

Old lawns are apt to be uneven and covered with worm casts and even mole hills, so when you start getting it into shape again, set the cutter at its highest position for the first two or three mowings. Then, if you can, run a roller over the lawn to level out the bumps and loose soil before you take a closer cut.

To tackle extra long grass, tilt the Lawnderette backwards and push it a few feet into the uncut grass. Lower the front edge gradually as you move the mower to and fro. When the machine is level, tilt it back again and tackle the next stretch of grass the same way.

CUTTING AROUND VERGES

When you are cutting close up to a grass verge you can let the cutter overhang the edge as long as you remember that with one wheel off the ground there will be nothing to prevent the cutter from tilting over and digging into the soil. You avoid this by pressing down on the handle to keep the weight of the mower on the rear roller.

When you start mowing with the Lawnderette you will notice that the cutter throws out the grass to your right as you walk forwards so in order to avoid spraying grass clippings over the flowerbed or path, always cut the margin of the lawn with the border or path on your left hand side so that the cuttings will fall on the lawn.

Bear this in mind also when you are cutting small areas of lawn by simply pushing the Lawnderette backwards and forwards and working it sideways across the area in a zig-zag pattern. If you work from right to left, you will leave the grass clippings behind on your right in a smooth layer and the cutter will only have to cope with the standing grass on your left. But if you work the other way, from left to right, the grass clippings will pile up and eventually choke the cutter. Even if they do not actually cause a hold-up, they will pile into untidy heaps that will spoil the look of the lawn and take a long time to wither away.

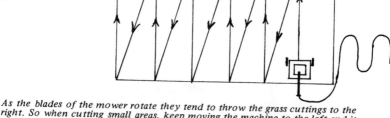

As the blades of the mower rotate they tend to throw the grass cuttings to the right. So when cutting small areas, keep moving the machine to the left and it won't get clogged with the grass you have just cut.

WHAT HAPPENS TO THE MOWINGS?

This is the first thing most people ask when they realise that there is no grass box on the Lawnderette, and if you have had to put up with the wearisome business of emptying the grass box of a conventional lawn mower you are bound to wonder where it all goes to. The answer is the Lawnderette is so light to handle and saves so much time that you can afford to cut the grass more often. When you do that the clippings are so fine that they practically wither away overnight.

A lot depends on your particular type of lawn grass, but broadly speaking you should set the cutter at High (1 1/4 in.) from the beginning of March up to the middle of April, Medium (1 in.) from then to the end of May, Low (3/4 in)., during June and July, going back to Medium up to the middle of September and High from then to the end of October. Used this way the Lawnderette will tend to keep down the tough, rank grasses while encouraging the more desirable growth. However, if you want to get a real lawn and not just a patch of grass, you will still need to carry out the normal lawn care of feeding, top dressing in autumn, weeding, aerating and so on.

TWO MOWERS: THE EASY WAY WITH LARGER LAWNS

The Lawnderette is all you need for the modest sized lawns that go with the average modern house on up to 1/4 acre of ground but older houses often have more ground and the lawns call for a bigger mower with a wider cut like the latest Black & Decker Lawnrovers. Even if you must have a big powerful machine for the bulk of your mowing, it is still worth while investing in a Lawnderette for the small islands of grass, steep banks, narrow paths and other places where handling the bigger machine is heavy work. It is a good idea, when you are using a big mower, to leave a strip 6 in.-12 in. wide around the edge to finish off with the small machine. This will prevent the weight of the big machine from crushing the unsupported edge of the lawn and making it difficult to trim afterwards.

In the past, experienced gardeners used a hand mower for these jobs; nowadays the Lawnderette at around the same price as a hand mower gets through the same work in a fraction of the time and with nothing like the hard labour.

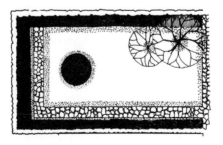

If you have a large garden which calls for a really big mower, the Lawnderette can cut down your mowing time and labour by taking care of verges and tricky places (shown shaded) where the big mower is too big or heavy to operate easily.

POWERED SHEARS AND EDGING TOOLS

In most gardens there are odds and ends of grass in places where you cannot use even a Lawnderette—up against walls, shrubs, the edge of the rockery and so on. Getting around these areas with a pair of hand shears, as with any of the various traditional tools for trimming the grass along the lawn edge, can be a slow, backaching operation. However, you can now get power tools for both these operations and as usual, they make an easier, quicker and better job of them. Mostly there are both mains and battery powered versions of each tool. If you use a mains operated tool already and have a long enough extension cable, the sensible thing is to go for the mains operated version. A battery powered tool is only worth while if you want to work a long way from the nearest power point. Although with battery powered tools you do not have to cope with a long cable, you have to keep the battery charged in and out of season and as a rule you do not have the reserve of power and all-day-long performance of a mains operated tool.

SAFETY

Never forget that all powered cutting tools are potentially dangerous both mechanically and if they are mains operated, electrically. At the same time, they are perfectly safe if you stick to the rules, and these are few and simple:

Never leave the tool unattended while it is still plugged in to the mains—even though the tool itself is switched off.

Never use the tool out of doors in damp conditions.

If you want to take a break in the middle of a job, unplug the tool at the cable connector and switch off at the mains socket. This is even more important if there are children around.

With most electrically operated shears and cutters it is a good idea to wear a belt and run the cable through a dog clip attached to it. This reduces the risk of cutting through the cable accidentally. (Another useful tip is to thread a length of garden hose over the last 6 ft or so of the cable so that it is impossible for it to get between the blades of the cutter).

THE BLACK & DECKER POWER GARDEN SHEARS

This is a mains operated tool that you can use for trimming shrubs and hedges as well as for tidying up the odd grass that you cannot reach with the mower. The business end of it is a 3-pronged cutter with one stationary and one oscillating blade giving a scissor action with 4,000 cutting strokes per minute. The power unit is double-insulated and housed in a moulded case with two handles, one the conventional pistol grip which incorporates the on-off switch and the other a large moulded ring which makes it easy to hold and operate the shears in any position. As it weighs only 4 lb you do not get aching arms from holding it up to trim laurels and other tall hedging shrubs.

With this class of tool you can do a lot of work close to the ground and in time the cutters may lose their keen edge. When this happens it is an easy matter to restore the edge with a file or carborundum slip or your Black & Decker Service Centre will exchange the blades for a reconditioned set for a small sum.

Electric garden shears like this one made by Black & Decker are useful for cutting grass in places out of reach of the mower and for trimming shrubs and small hedges.

THE BLACK & DECKER LAWN EDGER

Provided you start with a clean hard edge to your lawn, this tool can make a really astonishing difference to the job of trimming the grass fringe left by the mower. the cutter works on the principle of a circular saw. It rotates at 4,000 r.p.m. so you can trim the edge of your lawn at a comfortable walking pace. The power unit is double insulated and mounted on the side of the cutting guard. The assembly is supported on a sliding shoe and you push it along the edge of the lawn with a long handle, eliminating stooping and backache. (Some users find it easier to walk backwards with the edger instead of pushing it in front of them.) The pistol grip on the end of the handle incorporates the on-off switch and lock-on button. When the cutter needs sharpening you can either do it yourself with a file or carborundum slip or your Black & Decker Service Centre will exchange it for a re-sharpened cutter. If you have no convenient mains supply point there is a Black & Decker battery powered lawn edger something like the mains model. This tool is powered by a 6 volt rechargeable battery which will give about one hour's continuous cutting. Other manufacturers make battery powered models of both grass shears and lawn edgers. However, you must expect to pay more for a battery operated tool because the motor itself is more costly and you have to buy a battery and a charger. neither of them cheap.

Electric lawn edge trimmers take the sting out of one of the most tedious jobs in the garden. This Black & Decker model operates at 4,000 rpm and trims 100 ft per minute.

POWER TOOLS IN THE GARDEN:
HEDGE TRIMMING

Electric power has done more for hedge trimming than for any other job around the garden. You can cut more hedge with an electric trimmer in ten minutes than you can cut in an hour with hand shears. Most types of garden hedges need cutting at least three times a year and would benefit from cutting twice as often as that, so with the extra leisure time you gain it does not take many months for an electric hedge trimmer to justify its cost, which need not be very great.

Properly used, an electric hedge trimmer will not only do the job more quickly, it does it very much better. (Apart from anything else, it is easier to get a nice flat finish with a sweep of a fast cutting power tool than by nibbling away with hand shears). With a hedge trimmer you can pick up the knack of hedge cutting in half an hour whereas a lot of people use hand clippers for years and never learn to make a good job of it. However, this type of power tool is potentially dangerous both mechanically and electrically. This aspect is dealt with more fully under safety, above.

WHEN TO TRIM

When and how you should trim your particular hedge depends on a number of things such as the variety of hedging plant, its age, its position, the type of soil, the part of the country you live in and of course the weather over the year. It also matters whether you want to encourage the hedge to grow higher or wider, keep it the way it is, or reshape it. However there are some general hints on trimming that apply to most hedges:

Do not be afraid to trim hard around April if you are reshaping your hedge. All the common hedging plants are tough and soon recover.

Start trimming in late March or early April and at intervals of 3–4 weeks up to the end of September if you want the hedge to look tidy all the season. (You can leave privet and hawthorn as late as July.)

If you want to keep to the bare minimum then trim twice a year, in April and August.

Do not trim young hedging in the first year after planting.

If you want to reshape a hedge, cut it in April to 4 in. below the height you plan to have it.

If you want a hedge to grow higher or wider, trim only twice a year and cut back the new growth to within 2—2 1/2 in. of the level at last trimming.

For preference, shape the hedge so that it grows narrower towards the top.

Skim off any odd shoots that you see sticking up at the end of the autumn so that the whole hedge looks tidy through the winter and all the growth starts off level in the spring.

Holly and laurel hedges should be pruned with secateurs, not trimmed like other hedging.

Do not trim box hedges until all risk of frost is over.

HOW TO TRIM

One of the main reasons for cutting a hedge is to make it grow thicker so that it makes a more effective barrier and looks better. The two ways of doing this are by feeding it (your garden shop will advise you on the right kind of fertiliser) and by frequent cutting. Generally speaking, when you cut a growing stem it tends to put out shoots lower down, replacing the single stem you have cut with several new shoots. These grow out and fill the gaps in the surface, so within reason, the more often you cut a hedge the thicker it grows.

Even when you are in a hurry to grow a hedge taller and wider, you should still cut it often so that you will arrive at the final shape in stages even if it takes a year or two longer. That way your hedge will have a stiff, close texture instead of a few long straggly branches ending in tufts formed where you finally started to trimming it: so if you want a hedge to grow taller or wider, skim off the tips of the new growth from time to time instead of leaving it alone until it reaches the required height.

An established hedge is a different proposition. If it is already as tall and wide as you want, then you should keep it trimmed back to the level of the old wood. After a season or two you will find that the trimmer rides over the dense layer of old wood and shaves off the soft new shoots with very little need of guidance from you.

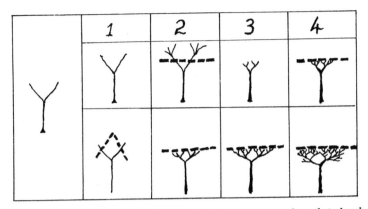

Frequent trimming makes a hedge grow thicker because growth tends to break out below the cut giving several new shoots in place of the original stem. The plant below has been cut twice as often as the one above so it grows thicker and spreads further.

When you cut a hedge with hand shears you are using one pair of cutting edges that only act in one direction; when you open them out to take another bite they just waste effort. An electric hedge trimmer has anything from 16 to 30 pairs of cutting edges and each pair cuts both ways at anything up to 4,000 strokes per minute. So you can see why an electric trimmer is so very much faster than hand shears.

The cutting performance of an electric hedge trimmer depends on the length of the blade (assuming the same number of cutting strokes per minute). You can buy electric hedge trimmers for normal garden use in blade lengths from about 12 in. to 24 in. The length you choose should depend on the amount of hedge you have to cut, not on its width or height. The object of extra length is to get through the job quicker and while it makes sense to buy a 24 in. model to save an hour on a long hedge, the extra cost and weight is not worth while on a hedge you could cut in 20 min. with a 12 in. model.

SINGLE OR DOUBLE EDGE

You can buy electric hedge trimmers with the cutting edge on one side of the blade only or with a cutting edge on both sides. The single edge models are cheaper but of course they will only cut on the forward stroke. If you miss any odd bits you have to waste time on the back swing to go over the same place again. With the double edge blade you can do the tidying up with the back edge when you swing back for the next forward cutting stroke. So you can get through the job quicker and with less wasted effort, but there is more to it than that.

When you sweep the hedge trimmer along the surface of the hedge, it meets shoots pointing in all directions. The cutter easily catches and slices through all the shoots that stand up or point backwards, but those that lie the way you are cutting just bend and let the cutter slide over them. If you use a single edge cutter and always work in the same direction, these shoots get missed every time and grow longer and longer. After a season or two you will find your hedge consists mainly of these long stems all growing the same way.

The answer, of course, is to cut the hedge in the opposite direction, but this is not easy with a single edge cutter. Either you have to lean over the hedge and cut it from the other side, or you have to turn the hedge trimmer upside down and risk cutting through the cable.

With a double edged trimmer there is no trouble; you simply swing the blade alternately backwards and forwards or up and down and you automatically trim all the shoots, no matter which way they are pointing. The result is a thick uniform growth that looks handsome and actually gets easier to cut season by season.

Top: A single edge hedge trimmer cuts always in one direction and tends to miss growth pointing away from it. Centre: You can help to prevent long straggling growth from developing by tilting the hedge trimmer down at an angle. Bottom: A double edge trimmer cuts both ways and provides the complete answer to the problem.

Black & Decker hedge trimming attachment for power drill.

THE BLACK & DECKER HEDGE TRIMMERS

The Black & Decker range of hedge trimmers includes two drill
attachments, four mains powered models a 12 volt battery-powered
model and a remarkable cordless electric trimmer powered by a light
weight rechargeabe battery housed in the handle. All models have
the same arrangement of electric motor and gearbox mounted at the
end of the cutter in a housing incorporating a pistol grip with trigger
on-off switch and lock-on button. And all but the cheapest mains
model are double insulated.

THE HEDGE TRIMMING ATTACHMENTS

There are two Black & Decker attachments for converting any of the
Black & Decker home user power drills into a hedge trimmer. Both
attachments are identical except that one has a 13 in. single edged
cutter while the other has a 16 in. double edged cutter and a small
extra cost.

To fit the attachment the drill chuck is first unscrewed and
replaced by the standard adaptor used for driving the other Black &
Decker attachments. This fits into a corresponding coupling on the
attachment. The attachment has a cradle to take the drill body and a
retaining clamp with lugs which engage the front ventilation slot on
the gearcase.

The pistol grip on the drill body forms one handle and a separate
moulded handle is mounted on the front of the attachment by a
bracket which you can adjust to the working position that suits you
best. The motor is controlled in the normal way by the on-off switch
and locking button on the drill pistol grip.

THE MAINS OPERATED SINGLE EDGE 13 INCH HEDGE TRIMMERS

There are two models, each with a 13 in. single-sided blade. The cheaper model has a moulded grip which can be screwed in to either side of the motor housing for right or left handed operation. This model is not double insulated and must be connected to the mains by a 3-core cable. It makes 3,000 cutting strokes per minute.

The second model works at 4,000 cutting strokes per minute and is fitted with a large, multigrip moulded handle. It is double insulated and needs only a 2-core mains cable.

THE MAINS OPERATED DOUBLE EDGED 16 INCH AND 24 INCH HEDGE TRIMMERS

Both double edged models are double insulated and fitted with the large multigrip moulded handle. The power units are identical but the 24 in. model is fitted with 50 ft of 2-core mains cable while the 16 in. model has a short lead with a 2-core connector.

THE 12 VOLT BATTERY OPERATED 13 INCH HEDGE TRIMMER

This model is similar to the cheaper 13 in. mains operated model but is fitted with a 12 volt motor which can be run off any 12 volt car battery. If you already have a 12 volt car battery that you could use, the makers supply a trolley which includes a junction box and extension cable to connect to the hedge trimmer: if you prefer a completely portable set-up you can have a lightweight battery kit which gives you two 6 volt batteries in a carry case with a shoulder sling and a mains operated battery charger.

THE CORDLESS POWER HEDGE TRIMMER

This model has obviously been designed with no thought to the final cost. The advertisements claim that it is 'the very best power hedge trimmer' and they are probably right. If you are not deterred by the fact that is probably the most expensive hedge trimmer, go and try one, but remember that once you have handled it you will be strongly tempted to buy it whether you can afford it or not.

The battery for this trimmer is housed in the handle so there is no loose cable to get in the way. A fully charged battery provides enough power to cut average hedging continuously for one hour or to cut 200 ft of hedge 3 ft high and 3 ft wide. If you want to cut more than this in a single session you can change over to a fully charged battery in a matter of seconds. The trimmer is supplied with a mains operated charger with plug-in sockets to take two batteries.

It will charge both batteries at once and is self adjusting to prevent overcharging even if it is left connected to the battery for weeks. It will fully charge a completely exhausted battery in 18 hours.

The trimmer has a double edged blade and has two handles one carrying the battery and the other moulded on to the top of the motor housing. A removable key is used for on-off switching. Without this key in position the trimmer cannot be switched on. In operation this model is no different from the ordinary mains or battery models, but the absence of a trailing lead and the double edged blade make it much easier to handle.

HOW TO USE THE POWER TRIMMERS

Before you start, give some thought to the shape of your hedge. Remember that with power hedge trimming you can tackle reshaping jobs that would be out of the question if you had to do them by hand. You may have a garden with a well established hedge and you may be happy to go on keeping it trimmed as it is, or maybe you would like to change its shape or cut it down to a smaller and more manageable size.

Before you do anything drastic ask advice, because some hedging shrubs will recover quickly from really hard re-shaping but others will either take a long time over it or even die off. Remember that the conventional shape straight with sides and flat top is not the only one. There is a lot to be said in favour of a pyramid-shaped hedge which you can cut in two instead of three operations. Any shape which narrows towards the top gives the growth near the ground a better chance to develop. Finally, there is no point in letting a hedge grow any higher than is absolutely necessary. A lot of hedges are too tall simply because in the past it was easier to let them grow their own way than keep them under control with hand shears. That sort of hedge can darken rooms and rob the garden of sunshine. So take a look at your hedge with this in mind and remember that an electric trimmer gives you the power to change it if you feel that way.

The best hedge shapes are the ones that narrow towards the top. Vertical hedges tend to put on more growth on top than at the sides and bottom.

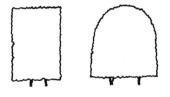

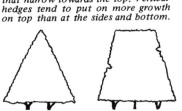

If the hedge runs alongside a lawn, mow the grass before you start to cut the hedge which will make it easier to sweep up the clippings. Before you switch on the trimmer see that the cable is well out of the way so that you can cut away from it and not towards it.

The trimmer leaves a neater finish if you tilt the cutting edge of the blade into the hedge at a slight angle so that it picks up growth pointing away from it. If you are working with a double edged blade, reverse the tilt as you sweep the blade back on the return stroke. It is easier to avoid carving out hills and hollows if you sweep the blade forward from the part already trimmed into the uncut growth. Start trimming a boundary hedge from the left hand end as you face the hedge and cut along the side with upward sweeps of the trimmer. The cable will then trail behind you well out of harm's way. When you reach the far end of the hedge, work back along the other side, in exactly the same way, with the hedge on your left and the cable trailing behind. You may feel happier if the cable passes over your shoulder and trails back; the important thing is to find the way that suits you and stick to it until it becomes automatic.

When you reach the opposite end and have trimmed both sides, you will be in the right place to start on the top. Now as you work from right to left along the top of the hedge the cutter will sweep over the trimmed surface and into the uncut growth. This trimming routine of course is the one recommended for a right handed person using a single sided cutter. It still applies if you are right handed and using a double edged cutter, because the natural tendency is to do most of the trimming with the left hand edge of the cutter, the way you swing a golf club or sweep up with a hand brush.

If you are left handed you will find the normal single edge cutter awkward to use because the motor and forward handle will stick into the hedge instead of being on the outside. However, with a double edged cutter you will have no trouble. Simply reverse the right handed directions given above and do your principal trimming with the other edge, that is the right hand edge as you look along the trimmer with the motor on top.

The 12 volt battery operated model is a single edge trimmer so if you are left handed you will have to go to a little extra trouble to use it right handed; or you can buy the double edged cordless model.

Follow this path when cutting a hedge and you won't run the risk of cutting through the mains cable.

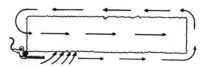

POWER TOOL ELECTRICS

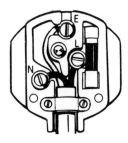

However your power tool is insulated, the final connexion to the mains will be by plugging it into a power point designed to take a 3-pin, flat pin, 13 amp, fused plug like this. The moulded rubber type is best. It is important to see that the correct fuse is fitted

There are two sorts of electric power tool: the normal type which you have to connect to the power point with a 3-core cable and the double insulated type which only requires a 2-core cable. The first type has a metal case which must be connected to earth so that if any of the live wires inside the motor or switch touches the case the mains current is carried away harmlessly to the earth and you do not get a shock. That is the job of the third wire in the 3-core cable.

The double insulated tool gets around the risk of shock in another way. In this type the case is either made of an insulating substance like moulded nylon or fibre glass or if it has a metal case this is completely covered with tough insulation. With this construction even if there is an electrical fault in the tool, the case cannot become live simply because it does not conduct electricity.

However, both types of tool have to be connected to the normal 3-pin power socket, so whether your power tool is earthed or double insulated, you fit the same sort of plug to the cable to connect it to the power point. The 3-pin rubber covered Duraplug stocked by most Black & Decker dealers is recommended for all domestic power tools. The terminals of these plugs are clearly marked to show you the right connexions for the *live* and *neutral* wires which are common to all power tool cables and the *earth* wire which is absent from the double insulated tools.

When you come to fit a plug to your power tool cable you can tell which wire is which by the colour of the insulation. Nowadays all electrical manufacturers use the same system of colour coding. However, this has only been so since 1971 and if your power tool was made earlier than that it will be coded differently. The table below tells you which is which under both systems.

Conductor	International Colour Code	British Colour Code up to 1971
Live	Brown	Red
Neutral	Blue	Black
Earth	Yellow and Green	Green

The terminals on the plug are marked L, N and E so no matter which colour coding you are dealing with you can connect the cable the right way.

The 3-pin plug you buy will be fitted with a cartridge fuse held by a spring clip connected to the line terminal. You will see this when you undo the centre screw and take the cover off the plug. The job of the fuse is to protect the power tool from being damaged if something goes wrong inside. If this happens the fuse blows before the current rises dangerously. You can buy fuses which will blow at 3 or 13 amps and you should choose a value at least double the working current which is shown by the figure in front of the A on the nameplate of your power tool. For example, if the figure on the nameplate is 1A, the you should fit a 3 amp fuse; if the plug has a 13 amp fuse fitted when you buy it, get the dealer to change if for a 3 amp. Never at any time make do with a fuse of too high a rating.

The nameplate on your power tool will also show the working voltage of the tool, e.g. 200–250 V. This should be the same as that of your electricity supply. Your dealer will normally sell you a tool with the correct working voltage for your district, but if you want to be sure, or if you have bought the tool by post, you will find your supply voltage printed on the electricity meter. Most places have alternating current mains, but if you are on direct current it will not matter because all home user Black & Decker tools are designed to run on either a.c. or d.c.

EXTENSION LEADS

Power drills, saws and other bench tools are supplied already fitted with a length of cable for connecting to the power point. This cable is long enough for all normal use indoors. Garden tools, however, are used at some distance from the power point and such tools are usually supplied with only a short length of lead and a connector. You buy the extension lead separately and only need to get enough for your own particular garden. Fitting a longer lead than you need would simply add to the cost and make the cable more difficult to handle.

If you want to operate any of the bench tools out of doors e.g. when you fit a hedge trimming attachment to your power drill, you can use the same type of lead. However, you have to remember that the electrical resistance of the cable lowers the voltage available to drive the tool. So there is a limit to the amount of extension cable you can use. The thinner and longer the cable, the higher the resistance. So a long extension cable needs to be thicker than a short one and the more current a tool needs to drive it the thicker the cable you have to use.

All this is summarised in the table below. It will save you a lot of headscratching because you just have to look up the description of the cable that fits the working current of the tool (see the nameplate) and your farthest working distance from your power point (pace it out). If you want to operate further from the power point than the distance covered by the table you should ask the advice of your local electricity board as this will call for special equipment outside the scope of this book.

Amps figure on nameplate	0 to 2.0	2.1 to 3.4	3.5 to 5.0	5.1 to 7.0	7.1 to 100
Distance (ft)	Rating of Cable (amps)				
25	6	10	10	10	18
50	6	10	10	10	18
75	10	10	10	10	18
100	10	10	10	18	18
200	10	10	18	18	—
300	10	18	18	—	—

The code numbers of the Black & Decker cables suitable for the above currents are:

6 amp—SM 1023   10 amp—SM 1019   18 amp—SM 1025

CABLE CONNECTORS

If you want to extend a 3-core cable fitted with the normal 3-pin 13 amp power plug you can join it to the extension cable with a matching rubber covered socket. This type of socket has outlets normally closed by a shutter which slides out of the way when you push the long earth pin of the plug into its hole. These sockets are only suitable for use in dry conditions. For working out of doors and particularly when the cable will lie on damp grass you need a waterproof connector. This has an in-line arrangement of pins and you cannot plug the pinned half into the normal power point. (Note: Never extend a 2-core cable by using 3-pin adaptors and plugs with the earth pin disconnected. You might be tempted to connect a tool fitted with an ordinary 3-pin plug to the cable. The earth connexion of the tool would then be useless, making the tool potentially dangerous if it should develop an electrical fault which rendered the case live.)

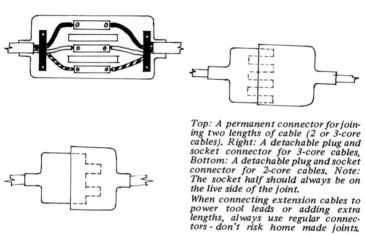

Top: A permanent connector for joining two lengths of cable (2 or 3-core cables). Right: A detachable plug and socket connector for 3-core cables, Bottom: A detachable plug and socket connector for 2-core cables. Note: The socket half should always be on the live side of the joint.

When connecting extension cables to power tool leads or adding extra lengths, always use regular connectors - don't risk home made joints.

By always connecting the socketed half on the mains side of the joint you make sure that there are no live pins exposed to cause accidents if you pull the connector apart while the extension cable is still connected to the mains at the other end.

Finally, if you want to use a bench tool both at the bench and in the open at the end of an extension cable fitted with a waterproof connector, you will have to make up two lengths of extension cable: a short one to let you connect the tool to the power socket at your bench and the long one to plug into the power socket when you connect the tool to the waterproof socket at the outdoor end.

Waterproof connectors are rubber covered and you can buy them for either 2- or 3-core cables. One half of the connector has either 2 or 3 projecting pins. (This half connects to the cable on the tool side) and the other half has corresponding sockets. (This half connects to the mains side.) When you push the pins into the sockets a rubber flange on one half overlaps the other half and forms a watertight seal. On the 3-pin type, for connecting 3-core cable, the centre pin lies off centre to make it impossible for you to connect the halves the wrong way round. It does not matter which way around you insert the pins of a 2-core cable connector because this type of cable is only used with double insulated tools.

STORING THE CABLE

If you just wind up your extension cable by hand like a ball of wool, you will be forever sorting out snarled and knotted tangles and leaving kinks that sooner or later lead to broken conductors. Experienced hands know the knack of picking up a cable in loops and giving the loops alternate right and left hand twists. This ensures that the cable will pull out from the coil without kinks because the alternate twists cancel each other out. You can arrive at the same result by snaking the cable on to the ground in a figure 8 and carefully storing it that way.

However, by far the best way to store cable is by winding it on to a drum like the Black & Decker Cable Reel.

THE BLACK & DECKER CABLE REEL

The Black & Decker cable reel is designed for the easy storage of Black & Decker extension cable for use with the whole range of home and garden power tools. It will hold up to 100 ft of either 2- or 3-core cable. The carrying handle is cranked to form an axle on which the drum turns and a winding handle on the side of the drum.

The cable is wound on to the drum with the 3-pin plug end on the inside and the waterproof connector on the outside, and the cable unwinds automatically as you walk back to plug in the 3-pin plug. This way the cable reel stays out of the way and leaves you free to work with the tool. You should always work with either the whole of the cable wound off the drum or no more than one layer left coiled on. This is because the resistance of the cable creates a certain amount of heat which must be free to escape. Otherwise the inside layers may get hot enough to soften the insulation and shorten the life of the cable.

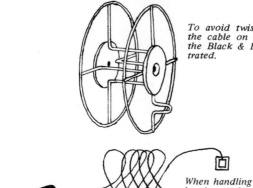

To avoid twists and snarl-ups, wind the cable on to a portable reel like the Black & Decker cable reel illustrated.

When handling lengths of loose cable lay it out in figure 8 double loops so that the alternate right and left hand loops will cancel out when the cable is pulled straight, leaving no twists or kinks.

ELECTRICAL MAINTENANCE

It cannot be said too often that you should always unplug any electric power tool from the mains supply before you carry out any adjustment, maintenance operation or repair—either electrical or mechanical.

When a power tool gives trouble, three times out of four the carbon brushes are to blame. There are two of these brushes, one on each side of the motor, secured by the two black plastic plugs screwed in at the back end of the motor housing. The brushes are held in contact with the commutator by light springs under the plastic plugs. If you unscrew the plugs with a screwdriver inserted in the slot you can remove the brush and spring.

The smooth running of the drill depends on good contact between the brushes and the copper bars of the commutator (which you can see by looking through the ventilation slots at the back end of the casing). As the brushes are made of carbon they gradually wear down and the harder you work the power tool the quicker they wear.

In normal use you should never need to look at the brushes, especially if you hand in your power tool for servicing, say once a year. If the tool is in constant hard use you might find it worth while to get a set of spare brushes from your Black & Decker Service Centre and fit them if the old ones have worn down 1/4 in. or look burned. If you are not absolutely sure that you can do the job correctly yourself you should get it done by your Black & Decker Service Centre.

Whenever you use a power tool for a job that creates a lot of dust such as sawing, sanding and drilling wood and plastics, some of it gets sucked into the ventilation slots at the back of the drill and in time can build up and restrict the flow of cooling air through the motor. This can cause the motor to overheat and could lead to trouble. So, from time to time, brush out the ventilation slots and as much of the windings and armature as you can reach with a narrow paint brush with long bristles. Afterwards flip the motor a few times to blow out the dust you have loosened.

RADIO & TV INTERFERENCE

All home user power tools using universal (a.c./d.c.) motors can cause interference with radio and TV reception. All Black & Decker home user power tools have special suppressors fitted to deal with this possibility. However, when a tool is new, or after fitting new carbon brushes you may notice some interference. This is the result of sparking at the brushes. You may actually see blue sparks through the ventilator slots when the tool is under load. However, as the brushes bed down both the interference and the sparking will clear up. A certain amount of sparking is always visible when the tool is working but this is normal and nothing to worry about.

In some areas the radio or TV signal is very weak. If you live in one of these areas your power tool may need an extra suppressor to cut out interference. Your Black & Decker Service Centre will fit this for a small sum.

PLANNING FOR POWER

Are you interested in power tools for the fun you get out of making things or because doing jobs yourself saves money on such things as house and car repairs? With most people it is a little of both, and starting with the right tools means more fun and bigger savings. That is why it pays to plan ahead before you buy your first power drill. Remember that it will be the basis of your whole working set-up. It will decide what sort of attachments you can safely add later and how well they will work for you.

Many people start by buying the cheapest and simplest tool. Then when they have had it for a short while and see its possibilities, for the first time they realise how much more they could do with a more powerful or versatile model. They then have the choice of cutting their losses and buying the model they should have had in the first place or being forever frustrated by working with a tool which is inadequate for the class or amount of work they want to do.

This need not happen to you, and as a basic guide do not forget that nobody ever regrets having bought the best. Bear in mind too that the trend nowadays, as costs go on rising, is all towards more owner repairing and jobs which you might not feel able to do at first, will look less terrifying when you have been using your power tool for a month or two. So make sure that when you graduate to the bigger jobs your equipment will be capable of it.

Do not buy the smallest single speed drill if you have an idea in a couple of years you will be wanting to do jobs and use attachments that call for a powerful 2-speed model. On the other hand, if the sort of thing you want to do is likely to call for a wide range of attachments to make furniture, toys, doll's houses, good quality wooden articles and so on, rather than having a lot of power to put up shelves, de-rust guttering and work with metal, then you would be better off with the appropriate integral tools or two or more of the less powerful drills, each one reserved for a particular attachment.

Black & Decker have provided for this last situation in the economy finishing sander. This in effect gives you a drill body without the chuck, fitted with the finishing sander attachment to which you can add any of the other attachments. One of these assemblies added to a separate single or 2-speed drill that you keep purely for drilling makes a versatile arrangement that avoids a lot of attachment switching in the middle of the job.

Once you have decided on your basic power unit you will begin collecting accessories and attachments, starting with a set of twist drills and perhaps flat bits and building up a kit in easy stages. You will be tempted to buy extras just as and when you need them which is a hit and miss process ending up in your never having exactly what you want when you want it. The alternative is to buy your drill with all the attachments and accessories you are likely to want in a ready-assembled kit.

THE BLACK & DECKER KITS

Black & Decker offer kits of this type covering the whole range of individual requirements from the occasional user right up to the thoroughly professional tool chest of the man who wants to do everything. These kits are complete down to the last of those odd components that you always forget when you are trying to do the job yourself, piecemeal. They provide a convenient way of starting a workshop at any level, knowing that you have all the tools for the job. And, incidentally, if any well-disposed member of your family circle is thinking of setting you up with a power tool and what goes with it as a Christmas or birthday present, they can do it this way without worrying over the correct choice of tools and accessories.

The Black & Decker power tool kits are detailed in the technical data section at the end of the book.

END PRODUCT

You do not buy power tools just to play with. The tool is just a means to the end product and that may be anything from a shelf in the kitchen to a suite of dining room furniture or an extension to your garage. This book is simply intended to give you a picture of what sort of electric power tools you can buy, what sort of things they do and how to use them; it does not attempt to tell you what to make, first because it would have to be a very big book to cater for everybody's needs and also because there is plenty of information on the subject on the shelves of every public library and in periodicals like *Do it yourself* Magazine and all the other general and specialised periodicals on woodwork, carpentry, house repairs and the like.

However, to get your hand in it is as well to practise on something that does not matter. A worthwhile item to make would be a suitable storage unit for your power tool and its accessories and attachments. Even if it is a rough job when you have finished it, you will be able to use it and that is better than over-reaching yourself at the start and producing an occasional table that your wife will not have in the house.

Start by making a carry-box that you can load with a selection of tools from your workshop for the job you have on hand. You could graduate to a full-sized tool cupboard and then a work bench. You might even build yourself a new workshop using plans from one of those books on woodworking in your local library. Finally, when you get around to tackling that occasional table your wife will probably pay your workmanship the compliment of a repeat order. She might even make you a present of a bigger and better power drill!

The following pages list the whole of the current range of Black & Decker power drills, attachments, integral power tools, power tool kits and accessories. Black & Decker manufacture a separate range of industrial power tools; the products listed here are all specifically designed for the home user.

No prices are given since these are always subject to change. The makers quote recommended prices for their products in their sales leaflets but they leave dealers free to fix their own selling prices and suggest that you should shop around before making a purchase.

SUPER D 500 3/8 in. DRILL
Single-speed 3/8 in. chuck. Drills 3/8 in. in steel, 1/2 in. in masonry, 3/4 in. in wood.

POWERDRIVER 5/16 in. DRILL
Single-speed 5/16 in. chuck. Drills 5/16 in. in steel, 3/8 in. in masonry, 5/8 in. in wood.

D 420 5/16 in. 2-SPEED DRILL
Slow speed 900 r.p.m., fast speed 2,400 r.p.m. 5/16 in. chuck. Drills 5/16 in. in steel, 3/8 in. in masonry and 5/8 in. in wood.

D 520 3/8 in. 2-SPEED DRILL
The most popular 2-speed drill. Slow speed 900 r.p.m., fast speed 2,400 r.p.m. 3/8 in. chuck. Drills 3/8 in. in steel. 1/2 in. in masonry, 3/4 in. in wood.

D 720 1/2 in. 2-SPEED DRILL
Has the extra capacity to drill 1/2 in. in steel, 3/4 in. in masonry, 1 in. in wood. Slow speed 900 r.p.m., fast speed 2,400 r.p.m.

D 820 1/2 in. 2-SPEED DRILL
A de-luxe drill with needle and ball bearings, nylon coating on die cast casing for added protection. Drills 1/2 in. in steel, 3/4 in. in masonry, 1 in. in wood.

D 640 5/16 in. 2-SPEED HAMMER DRILL
A 2-speed Hammer Drill specially designed to give efficient drilling in concrete and hard masonry. The hammer action is easily disengaged for normal drilling.

DNJ 74 3/8 in. 2-SPEED HAMMER DRILL
For drilling up to 3/8 in. in the concrete. Reverts to a normal 2-speed drill at the twist of a collar. Double insulated. Including carrying case with space for accessories.

DNJ 72V 1/2 in. MULTI-SPEED DRILL
Gear change drill with an accelerator, combining mechanical gear changing with variable finger-tip speed control. Double insulated. Including carrying case with space for accessories.

DN 70V 3/8 in. VARIABLE SPEED DRILL
With variable fingertip speed control from zero to 2,600 r.p.m. Double insulated. Including carrying case.

D 986 JIGSAW ATTACHMENT
For straight or intricate cuts in almost any material—wood, metal, plastic or asbestos. Complete with wood-cutting blade. Cutting capacity 1 in. softwood, 3/4 in. hardwood.

D 9324 SANDING, BRUSHING AND POLISHING PACK
Containing backing pad, wire cup brush, polishing bonnet and 3 aluminium oxide sanding discs.

D 978 SCREWDRIVER ATTACHMENT
Complete with bit and finder. Converts a powerdriver into a power screwdriver. Automatic clutch. Complete with bit and finder to drive Nos. 5 to 9 screws.

D 984 CIRCULAR SAW ATTACHMENT
Saws wood up to 1 1/4 in. thick. Adjustable for depth and angle of cut. Rip-fence included to ensure accuracy of cut. Complete with combination rip and cross-cut blade.

D 988 FINISHING SANDER ATTACHMENT
Makes short work of preparation for decorating and gives a smooth, professional finish to any 'do-it-yourself' job.

D 990 PORTABLE SAW BENCH
Converts a powerdriver and circular saw attachment into a fully adjustable power saw bench. Built-in protractor for mitring and rip-fence for straight cutting.

SAW TABLE (D 992)
Fits into a work bench to convert a powerdriver and saw attachment into a fixed saw table. Adjustable for depth and angle cutting.

D 994 24 in. LATHE
For centre and face plate turning. Complete with sliding tool rest, slotted face plate, fully adjustable head and tail stocks, driving centre and internal turning attachment.

D 982 13 in. HEDGE TRIMMER ATTACHMENT
Converts a powerdriver into a hedge trimmer to take the effort out of hedge trimming.

D 962 16in. SUPER HEDGE TRIMMER ATTACHMENT
Extra length double-edge blade.

D 980 HORIZONTAL DRILL STAND
Converts a powerdriver into a fixed power unit for easy grinding, polishing, wire-brushing and precision sanding.

DISC SANDING TABLE (D 998)
Clamps on to a horizontal stand or lathe head-stock for accurate sanding of flat surfaces, angles or curves.

GD 80 VERTICAL DRILL STAND
Converts a powerdriver into a highly accurate bench drill. Completely adjustable for height and radial swing.

D 590 HOME MAINTENANCE KIT NO. 1
A comprehensive kit containing the necessary tools for home maintenance, repair and decoration, in a custom built tool box.
 D 520 3/8 in. two speed Drill. Circular Saw Attachment. Finishing Sander Attachment. General Purpose Grinding Wheel.

Polishing Bonnet. Pkt. Sanding Discs (Medium). Horizontal Stand. Wire Cup Brush. Backing Pad. Wheel Årbor. Kit Box.

D 790 HOME MAINTENANCE KIT NO. 3
Contents as D 590 but with D 720 two speed 1/2 in. Drill.

D 540 POWERTOOL KIT
D 520 3/8 in. two speed Drill. Circular Saw Attachment. Saw Table. Finishing Sander Attachment. Buffing & Polishing Kit. Sanding, Brushing & Polishing Pack. Twist Drills. 25 ft Extension Cable. No. 8 Masonry Drill. No. 10 Masonry Drill. No. 12 Masonry Drill. Wood Augers. All contained in a custom built kit box.

D 760 POWER WORKSHOP
A comprehensive selection of powertools.

D 720 1/2 in. two speed Drill. Circular Saw Attachment. Finishing Sander Attachment. Sanding, Brushing & Polishing Pack. Jigsaw Attachment. Horizontal Stand. No. 8 Masonry Drill. Buffing & Polishing Kit.

All contained in a custom built kit box.

D 635 TWO SPEED MODERN HOMES KIT
A selection of powertools for the home handyman.

D 520 two speed 3/8 in. Drill. Circular Saw Attachment. Wire Cup Brush. Polishing Bonnet. Backing Pad. No. 8 Masonry Drill. Pkt. Sanding Discs (Medium).

D 535 MODERN HOMES KIT
Contents as D 635 but with D 500 S 3/8 in. single Speed Drill.

D 770 HOME BUILDER TOOL CHEST
A handsome wooden cabinet containing the tools you need for a complete home workshop.

D 720 1/2 in. two speed Drill. Circular Saw Attachment. Saw Table. Finishing Sander Attachment. Bench Stand. Horizontal Stand. Wire Cup Brush. Backing Pad. Sanding Discs (Fine). Sanding Discs (Medium). Sanding Sheets (Medium). Sanding & Sharpening Plate. No. 8 Masonry Drill. No. 12 Masonry Drill. Paint Mixer. Tube Disc Cement. 25 ft Cable. Set 4 Twist Drills. Set 3 Wood Augers. 3 Glass Screw Jars. 1 pr 6 in. Insulated Pliers. Spirit Level. Set Square. Folding Rule. 2 Plastic handled Screwdrivers.

D 330 6 in. CIRCULAR POWER SAW
Designed to cross-cut, rip-cut, slot, joint or rebate. Specialised blades also available.

D 315 POWER CIRCULAR SAW (ECONOMY LINE)
Saws wood up to 1 1/4 in. thick.

D 350 POWER JIGSAW
For straight or intricate cuts in hardwood, softwood, plastic, laminates, PVC sheet, asbestos, or metal. No-load speed 3,000 strokes per minute. Saws 1 in. hardwood, 1 1/2 in. softwood.

D 390 POWER FINISHING SANDER
For preparation in home decorating. Sands down paint, wood, plaster. 4,000 orbits per minute.

D 325 POWER FINISHING SANDER (ECONOMY LINE)
Gives a smooth finish to all carpentry and D.I.Y. jobs.

D 370 5 in. POWER GRINDER
A general purpose grinder. Cleans up edges on metal work. Sharpens drill bits and garden tools. Adjustable tool rest. 4,000 r.p.m.

POWER HEDGE TRIMMERS

D 450 13 in. POWER HEDGE TRIMMER
The hardened 13 in. blade works at over 3,000 cutting strokes per minute; weighs 5 1/4 lbs and has an adjustable grip for left or right hand working.

DNJ 450 13 in. POWER HEDGE TRIMMER
Double insulated. Weighs only 5 lbs. The 13 in. hardened steel blade works at 4,000 cutting strokes per minute. Wrap round handle.

DNJ 452 16 in. DOUBLE-EDGE BLADE POWER HEDGE TRIMMER
The extra length and double-edge blade cover a larger area of hedge. Double insulated.

DNJ 454 24 in. DOUBLE-EDGE BLADE POWER HEDGE TRIMMER
Extra long 24 in. double-edge blade and fitted with 50 ft of cable Double insulated.

MAINS-FREE HEDGE TRIMMERS

D 450B 12 VOLT HEDGE TRIMMER

Needs no direct mains supply, no extension cable, will work from any 12 volt supply. 13 in. blade.

12 VOLT BATTERY HEDGE TRIMMER PACK (D 458)

Needs no direct mains supply, no extension cable. Pack includes D 450B 13 in. hedge trimmer, two 6 volt batteries in lightweight carry case and a mains-operated battery charger.

12 VOLT BATTERY TROLLEY HEDGE TRIMMER PACK (D 459)

Enables you to use your own 12 volt car battery as the portable power supply. Kit includes D 450B 13 in. hedge trimmer, junction box and extension lead and a trolley to carry your battery.

CORDLESS POWER HEDGE TRIMMER (HD 1265)

For the gardener who wants the very best power hedge trimmer. Trims 1,300 sq. ft. at one charge. Power pack in handle. Mains-operated battery charger supplied with machine. Perfectly balanced, double-edge blade.

POWER LAWN MOWERS

THE D 484 LAWNDERETTE

Mains operated rotary mower. Adjustment for height of cut. Blade gives 12 in. wide cut and may be resharpened or replaced when worn. Double insulated motor with safety cutout to prevent overloading. Built in rear roller.

THE D 485 LAWNDERETTE

Economy model. Wheels at rear instead of roller.

ACCESSORIES

MASONRY DRILLS (INC. HAMMER TYPE)
No. 8.   Mas. D.8670; Ham.   51780
No. 10. Mas. D.8671; Ham. 996296
No. 12. Mas. D.8672; Ham.   51060

WOOD DRILLS
992945   Set of 4 twist Drills (1/16 in.,
         1/8 in., 3/16 in., 1/4 in.) in plastic
         wallet
990461   Set of 3 Wood Auger Bits
         (1/4 in., 3/8 in., 1/2 in.)

CIRCULAR SAW BLADES
D.7881   5 in. Combination Saw Blade
D.8002   5 in. Fine Tooth Saw Blade
D.999   6 in. Combination Blade

JIGSAW BLADES (PACKETS OF 3):
1365   Knife Blade
49493   Coarse, wood cutting
49492   Fine, wood cutting
49490   Coarse, metal cutting
49491   Fine, metal cutting
9489   General purpose blade

SANDING, BRUSHING AND POLISHING ACCESSORIES

U.1220   3 in. Wire cup Brush
U.1300   Backing pad with threaded shank
U.1302   Backing pad with 1/4 in. chuck shank
U.1310   Polishing Bonnet
U.1400   Metal Sanding and Sharpening Plate
U.2198   Tube of Disc Cement

5 in. ALUMINIUM OXIDE SANDING DISCS
(PACKETS OF 6):
U.1409   36 grit. Extra Coarse
U.1410   50 grit. Coarse
U.1411   80 grit. Medium
U.1412   120 grit. Fine

FINISHING SANDING SHEETS (PACKETS OF 12):
D.8500	36 grit. Extra Coarse
U.1413	60 grit. Coarse
U.1414	100 grit. Medium
U.1415	150 grit. Fine

BUFFING AND POLISHING ACCESSORIES
U.2206	Wheel Arbor (for use with the following):–
D.1109	3 in. General purpose grinding wheel
U.1201	4 in. Wire Wheel Brush
U.1320	3 in. Rag Buff
U.2199	Polishing Compound

GENERAL ACCESSORIES

U.1370	Screwdriver Bit, For No. 5 to 9 screws
U.1372	Screwdriver Bit. For. No. 8 to 12 screws
U.1509	Paint Mixer
994130	5 in. Medium Grinding Wheel (for D.370 Bench Grinder)
994131	5 in. Fine Grinding Wheel (for D.370 Bench Grinder)
D.1184	Jigsaw Adaptor Plate fits on to D.990 or D.992 to enable D.986 jigsaw Attachment to be used as a Saw Bench
D.589	Metal Tool Box
D.599	Cubic metal box

ROTARY HAMMER ATTACHMENT
D.968	For percussion action when drilling concrete or hard masonry

RIGHT ANGLE SPEED CHANGER
D.976

CABLE REEL
D.970	Holds 150 ft cable
D.973	Holds 100 ft cable

EXTENSION CABLE
3 core (with earth)
D.8382   25 ft
D.8384   50 ft
D.974   100 ft
2 core (without earth, for double insulated
units only)
D.975   50 ft
D.977   100 ft

GUARANTEE
If at any time* a Black & Decker product becomes defective due to
faulty workmanship or material, Black & Decker guarantee to replace
the defective parts free of charge.
*The Lawnderette Power Mower is guaranteed for 12 months.

SERVICE STATIONS
There is a national network of service stations where you can send or
bring any tool for servicing or repairs. The addresses can be found in
the Yellow Pages of your telephone directory or from your local
dealer.

USER ADVISORY SERVICE
For any advice you may require you can contact Black & Decker's
own special User Advisory Service at Cannon Lane, Maidenhead,
Berkshire.

Black & Decker reserve the right to alter the specification of the products in
this list.
   All powered units are available in 200/240 volts a.c. and are fully TV
suppressed.

METRIC EQUIVALENTS OF DIMENSIONS USED IN THIS BOOK

Although the engineering and other industries will have changed over to the metric system by 1975 the change will take longer to affect the home user power tool market. In the transition period you might find yourself having to use fractional drills to drill metric holes or metric drills to drill fractional holes. Sizes of other tools and materials used in the home and workshop will be affected in the same way. The following data on equivalents and conversions will be helpful when you are dealing with mixed units.

For everything but precision engineering it is enough to remember:

To convert Inches to Millimetres, multiply by 2.54.
To convert Millimetres to Inches, multiply by 0.39.

TWIST DRILL SIZES

Fractional twist drills used by handymen and in general jobbing work are manufactured in sizes increasing by 1/64 in. The table below shows only the 1/32 in. multiples since these are accurate enough for most home user drilling.

Metric twist drills are manufactured in steps increasing by .05 mm from .30 mm to 3.00 mm; by .10 mm from 3.00 mm to 14.00 mm and by .25 mm from 14 mm to 25 mm.

If you want the exact metric equivalent drill to a fractional drill size, you will not find one. You will have to accept the nearest standard metric drill which may be either slightly larger or slightly smaller than the exact drill size you want. To help you choose, the table below gives you the optional larger and smaller standard metric drills for each fractional drill size.

TWIST DRILL SIZES

INCHES		MILLIMETRES		
Standard Fractional Drill Sizes	*Decimal Equivalents*	*Nearest Equivalent Standard Metric Drill*		*Standard Metric Drills (mm)*
		Smaller	*Larger*	
1/32	.0312	.78	.80	
1/16	.0625	1.55	1.60	Sizes
3/32	.0938	2.35	2.40	0.32
1/8	.1250	3.10	3.20	0.35
5/32	.1562	3.90	4.00	and so on
3/16	.1875	4.70	4.80	in steps of
7/32	.2188	5.50	5.60	.03 mm to
1/4	.2500	6.30	6.40	3.00
9/32	.2812	7.10	7.20	–
5/16	.3125	7.90	8.00	3.00
11/32	.3438	8.70	8.80	3.10
3/8	.3750	9.50	9.60	and so on
13/32	.4062	10.30	10.40	in steps of
7/16	.4375	11.10	11.20	0.10 mm to
15/32	.4688	11.90	12.00	14.00
1/2	.5000	12.70	12.80	–
9/16	.5625	14.25	14.50	14.00
5/8	.6250	15.75	16.00	14.25
11/16	.6875	17.25	17.50	and so on
3/4	.7500	19.00	19.25	in steps of
13/16	.8125	20.50	20.75	0.25 mm
7/8	.8750	22.00	22.25	
15/16	.9375	23.75	24.00	
1	1.0000			